The Lord Is My Shepherd

and That's Enough

by
Jim Fellure

The Lord Is My Shepherd, and That's Enough
By Jim Fellure

Copyright © 2018 by Victory Baptist Press

ISBN: 978-1-940791-17-3

First printing, 2018
by Victory Baptist Press
Milton, Florida—USA

Proofreading by Heidi Berg
Layout and editing by Sarah Berg
Cover design by Trinity Lorimer

There is no claim to originality, and where recognition is not given, it is because we have no recollection or record of who said it first. If perchance a reader should find material published by himself, with no credit given, and would rather it not be used in this fashion, please contact the publisher, and a correction will be made in the next printing.

The naming of any person, movement, religion, or organization in this book does not constitute an automatic endorsement of their doctrines or actions.

All Scripture references are taken from the King James Version of the Scriptures, and all italics found therein are those of the translators. Where words or phrases are bold or underlined, it is for the emphasis of this author.

DEDICATION

To the beautiful young lady who, more than half a century ago (July 25, 1964), promised for better or for worse, in poverty and in wealth, in sickness and in health, to cleave only and ever unto me as long as we both shall live.

If love could keep her living,
she would never pass away.

To my wife Mary.

Contents

Preface vi

Acknowledgements vii

Part One
An Overview of the Psalter 1

Part Two
An Overview of Psalm Twenty-three 15

Part Three
A Devotional Commentary on Psalm Twenty-three 39

Psalm 23:1
"The LORD *is* my shepherd; I shall not want" 41

Psalm 23:2
"He maketh me to lie down in green pastures: he leadeth me beside
the still waters." 113

Psalm 23:3
"He restoreth my soul: he leadeth me in the paths of righteousness
for his name's sake." 133

Psalm 23:4
"Yea, though I walk through the valley of the shadow of death, I
will fear no evil: for thou *art* with me; thy rod and thy staff they
comfort me." 167

Psalm 23:5
"Thou preparest a table before me in the presence of mine enemies:
thou anointest my head with oil; my cup runneth over." 205

Psalm 23:6
"Surely goodness and mercy shall follow me all the days of my life:
and I will dwell in the house of the LORD for ever." 221

Bibliography 233

PREFACE

The writer has strived for a smooth flow of story, with each paragraph drawing the reader into new information relative to the subject at hand, and a desire to keep the narrative moving forward to a conclusion. So, redundancy and repetition are avoided as much as possible. However, when gleaning material from over fifty writers, with just about all of them taking the same overall view of our subject, but expressing it in different terms and illustrations, some redundancy or repetition was unavoidable to benefit from the light that each author provided.

ACKNOWLEDGEMENTS

In 1949, Reverend R. I. Williams, a pastor in Norfolk, Virginia, phoned the local paper to give them his sermon topic for the next day: "The LORD *is* my Shepherd," he said.

The person on the other end said, "Is that all?"

Reverend Williams replied, "That's enough."

The next day the church page carried his sermon topic as "The Lord Is My Shepherd—That's Enough!" and that misprint provided the title for this book.

My main source for information in this endeavor comes from more than half a century of reading what others have had to say about the Shepherd Psalm. However, this study would not have been a reality without the help of more than fifty audio sermons preached by a wide variety of serious students of the Psalms.

A final thank-you goes to Sarah Berg, our ministry perfectionist who oversees almost every book project Victory Baptist Press puts out, including this one, and also to Trinity Lorimer (if there was ever a person with natural-born graphics design capabilities, it would be her) for the cover design, and to Mrs. Heidi Berg, with her expertise in grammar, for proofreading the manuscript.

Part One

An Overview
of the Psalter

"What a record that would be, if one could write it down—all the spiritual experiences, the disclosures of the heart, the comforts and the conflicts which men in the course of ages have connected with the words of the Psalms! What a history, if we could discover the place the book has occupied in the inner life of the heroes of the kingdom of God!"

—Frederick Tholuck (1799–1877)

Most commentators divide the Old Testament into three major sections—those being history (the only totally accurate account of the past), prophecy (containing a view of the future), and the poetic books (containing the *feelings* of the writers).

Psalm 23 will ultimately be the focus of our study. However, Psalm 23 is not in isolation: it is a part of the whole, and just as one would not think of segregating one chapter out of a one hundred and fifty chapter book without first getting somewhat of an overview of the entire book, so it is with the Psalms.

A Unique Book

The book of Psalms (being the major poetic book) has the very unique position as the very centerpiece of the Bible. It also has the distinct privilege of being the largest book with 150 chapters. It contains the longest chapter (119), with 176 verses, the shortest chapter (117), with only 2 verses, and it is the only book that has only songs for its content with no chapter numbers.

Authorship

The book of Psalms has no proclaimed author, but according to the headings before many of the psalms, David composed as many as seventy-four of them. According to the electronic Online Bible, he composed seventy-five, and though Psalm 2 and Psalm 95 don't name the authors, Acts 4:25 and Hebrews 4:7 show David composed those as well, for a total of seventy-seven—just over half of the entire book of the one hundred and fifty psalms.

Psalms Promote Harmony

One preacher of the past had a habit of promoting *harmony in the home* with the idea of having good art, not modern abstract art, because good art is *harmony of colors.* Children should be taught good math (not new math) because good math is *harmony of numbers* and good music which is *harmony of sound.*

When David wanted to express his joy over brethren who dwelt together in unity, he wrote a psalm about it—"Behold, how good and how pleasant *it is* for brethren to dwell together in unity!" (Psalm 133:1).

One might get the idea that in order to have harmony among believers we must all be the same in every detail, but that is an erroneous idea. Harmony is simply when we use our differences to compliment, and not conflict. In a group of singers, regardless of how many different voices there may be, if one is off-key, out of tune, or has bad timing, it will cause discord. Harmony is created when our differences compliment each other, and the book of Psalms, with one hundred and fifty different parts, provides contrasts, but no conflicts, giving us a perfect example of harmony.

The First Hymn Book

Up until the eighteenth century, when Charles Wesley produced the first hymn book (1737), the Psalms were often referred to as a psalter, especially when bound into one volume by itself and used as Israel's song book and by most organized "Christian" denominations as their official and only songbook used in public worship.

Rowland E. Prothero wrote,

> To the Puritans of the seventeenth century, the Psalter was the book of books. Psalms were sung at Lord Mayor's feasts, at City banquets. . . . They were sung to "hornpipes" at rustic festivals. Soldiers sang them on the march, by the camp fire, on parade, in the storm of battle. The ploughman carolled them over his furrow; the carter hummed them by the side of his waggon. They were the songbook of ladies and their lovers, and, under the Commonwealth, the strains of the Psalms floated from windows in every street of Puritan strongholds.

> "Any one possessed of his five wits," writes Ambrose, "should blush with shame if he did not begin the day with a psalm, since even the tiniest birds open and close the day with sweet songs of holy devotion."

Prothero also said the Psalms have even had influence on American history. He wrote,

To gain liberty of worship and of psalm-singing, men and women crossed the seas, seeking in the New World the freedom that was denied them in the Old....

In July 1620, the Speedwell . . . lay at Delft Haven equipped for their transport to the New World. "When," says Winslow, "the ship was ready to carry us away, the brethren that stayed . . . feasted us that were to go, at our pastor's house . . . where we refreshed ourselves, after tears, *with singing of psalms*, making joyful melody in our hearts as well as with the voice.... And indeed it was the sweetest melody that ever mine ears heard."

To *the singing of psalms* the sails of the Mayflower were set to catch the winds that wafted the Pilgrim Fathers to the white sandbanks of Cape Cod; to their music were laid the foundations of the United States of America.

In 1787, it was to the 1st verse of Psalm 127 that Benjamin Franklin appealed, when speaking before the Convention assembled to frame a Constitution for the United States of America:—

"In the beginning of the contest with Britain, when we were sensible of danger, we had daily prayers in this room for the Divine protection. Our prayers, Sir, were heard, and they were graciously answered. All of us who were engaged in the struggle must have observed frequent instances of a superintending Providence. To that kind Providence we owe this opportunity of consulting in peace on the means of establishing our future national felicity. And have we now forgotten this powerful Friend? or do we imagine that we no longer need His assistance? I have lived for a long time (81 years), and the longer I live the more convincing proof I see of this truth, that God governs in the affairs of men. And if a sparrow cannot fall to the ground without His notice, is it probable that an empire can rise without His aid? We have been assured, Sir, in the sacred writings, that 'Except the Lord build the house, they labour in vain that build it'" [Psalm 127:1].[1]

Dr. John Ker described the Psalms as a "series of chambers where hearts and lives have left the records of their experience. They are very varied but all of them, prison or palace, this is the window toward the sun-rising."[2]

Herbert Lockyer, Sr., declares that

Multitudes of believers, not classed as heroes, have also found refuge in the dark and difficult hours of life in the majestic poetry of the Bible. . . . We can find verses from the Psalms quoted in strange places, and by unlikely lips. From sick beds, dungeons, scaffolds, lonely mountains and bleak moors; from poets, priests, and peasants; from exiles and martyrs come testimony to the comfort, encouragement and peace to be found in the language of the Psalms.[3]

In the commentary on the Psalms by Dr. John Phillips, we read,

---

1. *The Psalms in Human Life*, 173–175.
2. *The Psalms in History and Biography*, x.
3. *Psalms: A Devotional Commentary*, 11.

The Lord Is My Shepherd, and That's Enough

The Psalms are rich in human experience. At times they ring with the din and noise of battle, at other times they take us with hushed hearts into the inner sanctuary, into the immediate presence of God. At times they set our hearts aflame and our feet dancing for joy, at times we turn to them when our face is drenched with tears.

For the Psalms touch all the notes in the keyboard of human emotion. Here we have love and hate, joy and sorrow, hope and fear, peace and strife, faith and despair.[4]

Dr. Peter S. Ruckman declared the Psalms to be

For the saints, . . . THE devotional book of all time. It is the repository, the castle, the bomb shelter, the supply center, and the hospital to which they repair when wounded and bleeding, crushed by the world, the flesh, or the devil.[5]

"What is there," says St. Augustine, "which may not be learnt in the Psalms? Have we not proceeding from them the greatness of all virtue, the rule of justice, the comeliness of purity, the perfection of prudence, the pattern of patience, every good, in short, which can be named? The knowledge of God, the full prediction of Christ to come in the flesh, the hope of a common resurrection, the fear of punishment, the promise of glory, the revelation of mysteries, yea, all good things are hid and heaped

---

4. *Exploring Psalms*, Vol. 1, 11.
5. *Psalms Commentary*, Preface.

together in these psalms as in some great and public treasury."[6]

The following words come from Charles Herbert Morgan's very detailed and thought-provoking introduction to the Psalms—

It would intensely engage us and be a lure to reawakened study of the Psalter if we could know the exact order in time in which the hundred and fifty psalms were produced. In imagination we would then lay our steps beside the tiny streamlet of the psalm first written and would follow the meandering course of ever-widening waters until at the end its full tide flows forth to refresh and make fertile the field of human life. However, let no one suppose that such a strict chronology can be applied to the growth of the Psalter. Rather, we should understand that some of our present psalms have gushed and trickled and oozed out of hidden springs and reservoirs of earlier Hebrew psalmody, so that their real beginnings can never be traced.

Nor can their endings be calculated. They are still growing in their power to interpret, guide, and bring near to God human hearts in their aspirations, duties, problems, and sorrows.

In the Psalms all elements of human nature and experience become revealing and ministrant. . . . All the frailty, weakness, doubt, fear, discontent, envy, jealousy, complaining, desperation, madness, folly, pride, sin, and

6. Kennedy, *The Psalter, or Psalms of David, in English Verse*, xxi–xxii.

wickedness of man can be found unfolded in the Psalms. No less can one discover man's nobility, likeness to the angelic and divine, faith, prayerfulness, strength, courage, purity, patience, humility, uprightness, honor, truth, and goodness. In the Psalms man is a creature of the dust, destined to death, his life fleeting as a wisp of cloud dissolving in warm air; but he aspires to know the God who inhabiteth eternity, and to dwell with him evermore. He is pictured under every condition of this life: a king; a royal bridegroom; a soldier; a fugitive hunted in the wilderness; a stranger, suspected and oppressed; a friend and acquaintance, slandered and betrayed; a captive exile, having no heart to sing his loved psalms in a distant land; a sick sufferer, tossing on a hard couch through the night watches; a citizen, honest, clean, and incorruptible; a sailor, buffeted and storm-driven; a farmer, rejoicing beside the full threshing-floor; a happy householder, with wife and children about the table; a pilgrim, with the memory of sweet lodging-places on the way to Zion; a time-forgetting, absorbed worshiper in the central sanctuary of his people. Reaching up through man's natural experiences and qualities, the Psalms portray transcendent suffering, sacrifice, and service, aiming at human and divine concord, and pointing forward to Christ the Messiah.

But, beyond all else, the Psalms can be our daily companions because they carry a wonderful disclosure of God.

The writers of the Psalms never hesitate to make use of concrete and mundane figures, and to place side by side those that present widely different pictures to the mind's eye. God is a towering "rock," and his favored servant abides "under the shadow of the Almighty." God tenderly broods us, and to the hapless child of earth the assurance is given that "he shall cover thee with his feathers." God is a "sun," and like the luminary of day, he will cause his "face to shine upon us." These and countless other figures bodying forth God to our finite thought never obscure the radiant truth of His personality. "More persistently than any other book in the Bible does the Psalter bring home to us the overwhelming sense of the reality and the personality of God" [McFayden, *The Messages of the Psalmists*, 5]. "The chief service which the Psalms have rendered to the religion of the world is the preservation of the idea of the living God, without any impairing of his absolute and inconceivable glory. . . . No sacred book of any nation has solved this fundamental problem of all religion, how to preserve at the same time the infinity and the personality of God, as has the Psalter"[*Hast. Bib. Dict.*, IV, 157].

The focal point of the teaching of the Psalms about God is the same as that of the New Testament as presented by Paul. He solves the whole mystery of salvation, as far as it can be solved, by showing that two things hold together in God: his righteousness and his mercy. The

11

same beautiful accord of these two things in God appears in the Psalter. . . .

As a last thought we should note that the leading or most vital psalms are so emancipated from the local and racial and are so universal in their appeal that they cannot be assigned to a particular date or set of circumstances. They are companionable and at home in our century. In proof that they are timeless we may take the impressions made upon great souls by the Psalms. "The Psalms have been called . . . the summary of both Testaments." "These flowers can be carried to every clime and every soil, and they bloom in fresh youth. It is a book of song for all ages." "The Psalms were meant for all time. Other things grow old, but these do not. Other things die, but these live. Cut across the arteries of their life anywhere, and they bleed." "Songs which like the Psalms have stood the test of three thousand years may well be said to contain in them the seed of eternity." "If it is a peculiarity of the classic that the oftener it is read the more beautiful and full of meaning it becomes, then are the Psalms classic in the highest degree." Let Gladstone conclude these testimonies to the truth that the Psalms are free from the fetters of space and time, and therefore are at home in America in the twentieth century as much as in the Roman empire in the first, and that they are myriad-voiced and myriad-toned in their message. "In the book of Psalms there is the whole music of the heart when touched by the hand of the Maker, in all its tones that whisper or that swell, for every hope and fear, for every joy and pang, for every form of strength and languor, of disquietude and rest. All the wonders of Greek civilization heaped together are less wonderful than is the simple book of Psalms."[7]

As further testimony to the hope, encouragement, and help for every situation in life from the cradle to the grave, and beyond the grave, most New Testaments, especially those used by personal workers who intend to give them as a gift to the person they are dealing with, when bound in a single volume will include the Psalms.

---

7. *The Psalms as Daily Companions*, 3, 6-10.

Part Two

An Overview of Psalm
Twenty-three

Writers who study Old Testament theology tell us there are at least ten different compound names, or descriptive titles, for Jehovah found in the Scriptures.

Three of those Hebrew phrases are still recorded in our English Bible (Jehovahjireh, Jehovahnissi and Jehovahshalom—Genesis 22:14, Exodus 17:15, and Judges 6:24), and the other seven are very easily found. A comparison of each description of what is said about Jehovah in the Old Testament is also said of Christ in the New Testament, showing very clearly Jesus Christ was God in the flesh.

Jehovahjireh—"the God that sees and provides"
(Genesis 22:13–14)

Applied to Christ in Philippians 4:19—"But my God shall supply all your need according to his riches in glory by Christ Jesus." (See also Ephesians 3:20.)

Jehovahnissi—"Jehovah is my banner"
(Exodus 17:8–13. See also Isaiah 13:1–5)

Applied to Christ in 1 Corinthians 15:57—"But thanks *be* to God, which giveth us the victory through our Lord Jesus Christ."

Today when a victory is won we might say "Fly your flag," but in the words of days gone by they would say, "**Raise the banner**." We even enjoy singing the old 1800s song by William Sherwin—

> Rouse, then, soldiers! **rally round the banner**!
> Ready! steady! pass the word along;
> Onward! forward! shout a loud hosanna!
> Christ is Captain of the mighty throng.

Jehovahshalom—"Jehovah is peace"

(Judges 6:24)

Applied to Christ in Ephesians 2:14–15—"For he is our peace, who hath made both one, and hath broken down the middle wall of partition *between us*; Having abolished in his flesh the enmity, *even* the law of commandments *contained* in ordinances; for to make in himself of twain one new man, so making peace." (See also Philippians 4:9.)

"The LORD that healeth thee"

(Exodus 15:26)

Applied to Christ in Matthew 4:23—"And Jesus went about all Galilee, teaching in their synagogues, and preaching the gospel of the kingdom, and healing all manner of sickness and all manner of disease among the people." (See also Matthew 12:15; 14:14.)

18

"THE LORD OUR RIGHTEOUSNESS"
(Jeremiah 23:6)

Applied to Christ in 1 Corinthians 1:30—"But of him are ye in Christ Jesus, who of God is made unto us wisdom, and righteousness, and sanctification, and redemption."

"The LORD *is* there"—the God of presence
(Ezekiel 48:35)

Applied to Christ in Matthew 1:23—"Behold, a virgin shall be with child, and shall bring forth a son, and they shall call his name Emmanuel, which being interpreted is, God with us." (See also Hebrews 13:5 and Revelation 21:1–3.)

"The LORD that doth sanctify you"
(Exodus 31:13)

Applied to Christ in 1 Corinthians 1:30—"But of him are ye in Christ Jesus, who of God is made unto us wisdom, and righteousness, and sanctification, and redemption."

"The LORD of hosts"
(1 Samuel 1:3; 17:45)

Applied to Christ in Hebrews 2:10—"For it became him, for whom *are* all things, . . . in bringing many sons unto glory, to make the captain of their salvation perfect through sufferings."

"God of gods, and Lord of lords"
(Deuteronomy 10:17, Joshua 22:22, and Daniel 2:47; 11:36)

Applied to Christ in Revelation 19:16—"And he hath on *his* vesture and on his thigh a name written, KING OF KINGS, AND LORD OF LORDS."

These nine descriptive names of Jehovah clearly show He was all humanity needed for any and every situation in life. Likewise, we Christians can read the same descriptions of Jesus Christ and come to the conclusion that regardless of how critical a situation we find ourselves in, He being none other than Jehovah **God in the flesh** is all, and even more than we need!

The critics of Christianity will object to the truth that Jesus Christ was God in the flesh because we offer no biological proof of how it happened, but may I remind the reader that "without controversy great is the **mystery** of godliness: **God was manifest in the flesh**" (1 Timothy 3:16).

The story was told of an agnostic coming to hear one of our great American statesmen, William Jennings Bryan, speak. To the best of my memory, the story says that after the meeting was over the agnostic approached Bryan and asked, "Do you believe that Jesus was God?"

To which Bryan replied, "I most assuredly do!"

The agnostic then said, "Can you explain, or at least illustrate how Jesus could have been God?"

Bryan said "No, I cannot."

The agnostic replied, "How can you receive or believe in someone that you cannot understand with natural and rational thinking?"

20

Bryan replied, "Sir, so keenly aware am I of the fact that I am a sinner that I realize I must have one beyond my intelligence to be my Saviour."

Dr. Monroe Parker told a similar story about a brilliant lawyer coming to hear him preach and a similar conversation taking place. The lawyer just could not believe in the deity of Christ without some scientific proof, and Dr. Parker offered none because there is no analogy of God (you cannot analyze Him), so the lawyer went away without trusting Christ.

The next morning at breakfast Dr. Parker's little boy asked, "Daddy, is Jesus God?"

"Yes son, Jesus is God."

"Daddy, is Jesus the Son of God?"

"Yes son, Jesus is the Son of God."

"Daddy does that mean that Jesus is Jesus' son?"

And Dr. Parker very wisely said, "Son, there are some things that we cannot explain or understand without the Bible, and the Bible does say that Jesus is God and at the same time He is the Son of God. That's what the Bible says!"

The boy replied "Oh, I see!"

At that point Dr. Parker said he thought of the verse where Jesus said, "Verily I say unto you, Whosoever shall not receive the kingdom of God as a little child shall in no wise enter therein" (Luke 18:17).

That very night the lawyer returned to hear Dr. Parker preach again. At the conclusion of a simple salvation message, the lawyer came forward and in simple faith trusted Christ as his own Lord and

Saviour. The next morning Dr. Parker and the lawyer had breakfast together, and during the course of their time together the lawyer said, "How could anyone be so naïve as to doubt the deity of Christ?"

Now, just as Jehovah embodied Himself into one person in the New Testament—the Lord Jesus Christ—and meets all of our needs through Him, He has also condensed all of the nine descriptive phrases concerning His provision for mankind into one phrase—

"The LORD *is* my shepherd"

(Psalm 23:1)

This is applied to Christ in John 10:11, where Jesus said, "I am the good shepherd."

Now we come to find all the nine benefits and blessings of the Shepherd described in the six short verses that make up this great psalm.

He is the God that sees and provides—

"He maketh me to lie down in green pastures." (v. 2)

He is the God that gives victory in battle—

"Thou preparest a table before me in the presence of mine enemies." (v. 5)

He is the God that gives peace—

"He maketh me to lie down." (v. 2)

He is the God that brings healing—

"He restoreth my soul." (v. 3)

He is the God that makes us righteous—

"He leadeth me in the paths of righteousness." (v. 3)

He is the God that abides with us—

"Thou *art* with me." (v. 4)

He is the God that sanctifies—

"The LORD *is* my shepherd." (v. 1)

"My shepherd" signifies ownership. If He is my Shepherd, then I am His sheep. I have been sanctified, or set apart, for the Shepherd's use.

He is The LORD of hosts: our leader, our captain—

"He leadeth me." (v. 2)

He is God of gods—

"The LORD" (v. 1)

> Christ is all I need,
>
> . . . .
>
> For me He died,
> On Calvary.
> This is why I know
> That He loves me so,
> Christ is all I need.

The Location of Psalm 23

Even the location of this psalm tells us it covers New Testament Christianity.

F. B. Meyer declared,

> This psalm has sometimes been called the Psalm of the Crook. It lies between the Psalm of the Cross and the Psalm of the Crown. If the Twenty-second tells of the Good Shepherd, who died, and if the Twenty-fourth tells of the Chief Shepherd, who is coming again, the Twenty-third tells of the Great Shepherd, who keeps His flock with unerring sagacity [wisdom] and untiring devotion.[1]

The prince of preachers, C. H. Spurgeon, said,

> The position of this psalm is worthy of notice. It follows the twenty-second, which is peculiarly the Psalm of the Cross. There are no green pastures, no still waters on the other side of the twenty-second Psalm. It is only after we have read, "My God, my God, why hast thou forsaken me?" that we come to "The LORD *is* my Shepherd." We must by experience know the value of blood shedding, and see the sword awakened against the Shepherd, before we shall be able truly to know the sweetness of the Good Shepherd's care.[2]

J. R. Miller, in his book *Perfect Peace,* published in 1902, said it like this,

---

1. *Shepherd Psalm*, 8.
2. *The Treasury of David*, Vol. 1, 353.

The Twenty-third Psalm nestles in the shadow of the twenty-second, like a quiet vale at the mountain's foot! It shows us a picture of perfect peace. We see the shepherd leading his flock beside the still waters and making them lie down in the green pastures. Even in the deep valley there is no gloom, for the shepherd walks with his sheep and quiets all their fears. This sweet shepherd psalm could come nowhere but after the Psalm of the Cross.

The Time of the Writing

Some writers believe the reference to dangers and hardships in the passage is an indication David was older and more experienced with tragedies than a younger man would have been—therefore more qualified to pen these words.

One writer declared that "no youth could have penned such words, no *sheltered life* could have given us such deep thoughts."

Those who hold such a position are forgetting that David, while living such a "*sheltered life*," also slew a lion, a bear, and a giant, and in his own words the reason he was not devoured by the beasts or the bully was because "The LORD . . . delivered me [him] out of the paw of the lion, and out of the paw of the bear," and when he faced Goliath he said, "This day will the LORD deliver thee into mine hand" (1 Samuel 17:37, 46). If God gave those victories to "little-boy" David while he was minding his father's sheep, He could also have given him the very words of this short psalm.

Another good illustration of what even a child, with the help of the Lord can do, that they could not do otherwise, is found in the life

25

of the blind hymn writer, Fanny Crosby. At only eight years of age, she wrote,

> Oh, what a happy soul am I,
> Although I cannot see,
> I am resolved that in this world
> Contented I will be.
> How many blessings I enjoy
> That other people don't!
> To weep and sigh because I'm blind,
> I cannot, and I won't.

Although we cannot say with absolute assurance when this psalm was penned, we can show a very distinct difference in the attitude of the writer between the days of him minding his sheep and the days of him ruling as king. In his old age when he was the king, he wrote and described some of the sorrows and heartaches he faced.

Consider this one psalm showing David's attitude in his senior years—

Give ear to my prayer, O God; and hide not thyself from my supplication. Attend unto me, and hear me: I mourn in my complaint, and make a noise; Because of the voice of the enemy, because of the oppression of the wicked: for they cast iniquity upon me, and in wrath they hate me. My heart is sore pained within me: and the terrors of death are fallen upon me. Fearfulness and trembling are come upon me, and horror hath overwhelmed me. And I said, **Oh that I had wings like a dove!** *for then*

would I fly away, and be at rest. Lo, *then* **would I wander far off,** *and* **remain in the wilderness**. Selah. (Psalm
55:1–7)

Spurgeon made an interesting comment on David's words, "Oh
that I had wings like a dove! *for then* would I fly away, and be at
rest. Lo, *then* would I wander far off, *and* remain in the wilderness"
(v. 6–7)—

> If he could not resist as an eagle, he would escape as
> a dove. Swiftly and unobserved, on strong, untiring pin-
> ions would he hie [haste] away from the abodes of slan-
> der and wickedness.[3]

A quick summary of this one psalm shows us that being elevated
to a higher position, even to the top of the ladder and living among
the multitudes of the big city, brought with it much crime, danger,
slander, opposition, and hatred, so much so that David would have
liked to flee into the wilderness, a place that, according to another
psalm ascribed to David, offered peace and tranquility, and a place
of pastures for the flock.

We read,

> Thou visitest the earth, and waterest it: thou greatly
> enrichest it with the river of God, *which* is full of water:
> thou preparest them corn, when thou hast so provided for
> it. Thou waterest the ridges thereof abundantly: thou set-
> tlest the furrows thereof: thou makest it soft with show-
> ers: thou blessest the springing thereof. Thou crownest
> the year with thy goodness; and thy paths drop fatness.

---

3. *The Treasury of David*, Vol. 1, (part 2) 446.

They drop *upon* the **pastures of the wilderness**: and the little hills rejoice on every side. **The pastures are clothed with flocks**; the valleys also are covered over with corn; they shout for joy, they also sing. (Psalm 65:9–13)

When the context of all the verses is considered, it shows what King David would really like to have done was to go back to the wilderness and watch over some sheep.

A simple, little incident in the life of a young lady in upstate New York illustrates how being promoted or moving up the ladder is not always the way we thought it would be.

As a young adult, while she was stranded in a very strong, winter blizzard and sitting by herself by the highway waiting for someone to come and rescue her, she sent a text message to her father saying, *"Why can't I just come home and go back to being a little girl? This adult life is tough!"*

Though David was in a much more severe situation than being stranded in a blizzard, his attitude seemed to be, "This thing of growing old and being king is tough. If I could, I would just go back to the wilderness and be a shepherd boy."

David's attitude here certainly does not fix the date of composing this psalm, but as an older man and serving as king, most of his psalms were about wars, heartaches, and sorrow. Even Spurgeon, who was not adamant about the time of its writing, made it a possibility that David was still a shepherd boy when he composed this Twenty-third Psalm. He wrote,

Sitting under a spreading tree, with his flock around him,
like Bunyan's shepherd-boy in the Valley of Humiliation,

we picture David singing this unrivalled pastoral with a
heart as full of gladness as it could hold.[4]

Though we do not know for certain the exact time of its writing,
there is one thing we do know for sure, "All scripture *is* given by
inspiration of God," and "holy men of God spake *as they were* moved
by the Holy Ghost" (2 Timothy 3:16, 2 Peter 1:21). Psalm 23, being a
part of the divinely inspired Scriptures, makes it imperative that we
believe God spoke to and through David.

One writer expressed the probability that while David as a young
lad was simply spending the day as usual, watching over his sheep,
the Lord spoke to his heart and said, "David, did you know that the
way you are watching over those sheep is the same way I watch over
you, and just as you make sure all their needs are met is the same way
I supply all your needs. And David, just as those sheep are not afraid
of any evil as long as you are with them is the same way I comfort
you with my presence. And David, just as those sheep have no fear
of you ever forsaking them in the wilderness, you have no fear that I
will ever leave you alone in this world."

David could have said, "Lord, I never looked at it like that. Right
before my very eyes, at all times has been a perfect picture of the way
you watch over and take care of me. I see it well." At that point the
LORD might have said "David, write it down," and David grabbed a
quill, an inkhorn, and a piece of parchment and wrote,

The LORD *is* **my** shepherd; **I** shall not want. He maketh
me to lie down in green pastures: he leadeth **me** beside
the still waters. He restoreth **my** soul: he leadeth **me** in the

4. *The Treasury of David,* Vol. 1, 353.

paths of righteousness for his name's sake. Yea, though **I** walk through the valley of the shadow of death, **I** will fear no evil: for thou *art* with **me;** thy rod and thy staff they comfort **me.** Thou preparest a table before **me** in the presence of **mine** enemies: thou anointest **my** head with oil; **my** cup runneth over. Surely goodness and mercy shall follow **me** all the days of **my** life: and **I** will dwell in the house of the LORD for ever.

While trying to establish a time for the writing of this psalm, at best we can only give circumstantial evidence to support our position, and we must exercise some caution in trying to prove something God had a reason for not telling us. We have a tendency, if a passage is too exact, to lock the interpretation and application into the very location and situation in which the events took place, but when they are ambiguous ("of words or other significant indications: admitting more than one interpretation, or explanation; of double meaning, or of several possible meanings")[5] they become timeless and instructive for all generations, which is the nature of the Psalms.

What Others Have Said

Spurgeon declared,

> This is the pearl of Psalms whose soft and pure radiance delights every eye. . . . Of this delightful song it may be affirmed that its piety and its poetry are equal, its sweetness and its spirituality are unsurpassed.

---

5. *The Oxford English Dictionary*, 2nd ed.

It has been said that what the nightingale is among birds, that is this divine ode among the Psalms, for it has sung sweetly in the ear of many a mourner in his night of weeping, and has bidden him hope for a morning of joy. I will venture to compare it also to the lark, which sings as it mounts, and mounts as it sings, until it is out of sight, and even then is not out of hearing.[6]

Henry Ward Beecher said this psalm is

the nightingale of the Psalms. It is small, of a homely feather, singing shyly out of obscurity; but, oh! it has filled the air of the whole world with melodious joy, greater than the heart can conceive. . . .

It has charmed more griefs to rest than all the philosophy of the world. . . . Nor is its work done. It will go singing to your children and my children, and to their children, through all the generations of time; nor will it fold its wings till the last pilgrim is safe, and time ended; and then it shall fly back to the bosom of God, whence it issued, and sound on, mingled with all those sounds of celestial joy which make Heaven musical forever.[7]

Author John Phillips offered these good words about this great psalm—

Of all the ways we can divide this psalm, I like best the one I found in my mother's open Bible, there beside her bed, the day after she died. Alongside this psalm she

---

6. *The Treasury of David*, Vol. 1, 353.
7. *Life Thoughts*, 11–12.

had written: "The secret of *a happy life, a happy death, a happy eternity.*"[8]

F. B. Myer declared,

One thinker at least, wearied with the perplexing questions that agitate so many hearts and brains in this
strange questioning age, and pressed to give some posi-
tive affirmation of his creed, began reciting these words
with solemn pathos of voice and kindling rapture of eye.
And when he had finished the whole psalm he added:
"That is my creed. I need, I desire no other. I learned it
from my mother's lips. I have repeated it every morning
when I awoke, for the last twenty years. Yet I do not half
understand it; I am only beginning now to spell out its
infinite meaning, and death will come on me with the
task unfinished. But, by the grace of Jesus, I will hold on
by this psalm as my creed, and will strive to believe it,
and to live it; for I know that it will lead me to the cross,
it will guide me to glory."

. . . As one looking into some priceless gem may see
fountains of colour welling upward from its depths, so,
as we shall gaze into these verses, simple as childhood's
rhymes, but deep as an archangel's anthem, we shall see in
them the gospel in miniature, the grace of God reflected
as the sun in a dewdrop, and things which eye hath not
seen, nor ear heard, nor the heart of man conceived.
Read into these words the meaning of the Gospels, and

8. *Exploring Psalms*, Vol. 1, 175.

you have an unrivalled creed, to which all Christians may unhesitatingly assent. . . .

It has remanded to their dungeon more felon [wicked] thoughts, more black doubts, more thieving sorrows, than there are sands on the seashore. It has comforted the noble host of the poor. It has sung courage to the army of the disappointed. It has poured balm and consolation into the heart of the sick. It has visited the prisoner and broken his chains, and . . . it has made the dying Christian slave freer than his master, and consoled those whom, dying, he left behind mourning, not so much that he was gone as because they were left. . . .

It is an oasis in the desert; it is a bower on a hill of arduous climbing; it is a grotto in a scorching noon; it is a sequestered arbour for calm and heavenly meditation; it is one of the most holy places in the temple of Scripture. Come hither, weary ones, restless ones, heavy-laden ones; sit down in this cool and calm resort, while the music of its rhythm charms away the thoughts that break your peace. How safe and blessed are you to whom the Lord is Shepherd![9]

Meyer also said that, in Psalm 23, "every sentence is a word-picture, painting in strong and vivid outlines some new scene in our earthly pilgrimage."[10]

---

9. *Shepherd Psalm*, 8-10.
10. Ibid, 71.

Jewish Rabbi Rami Shapiro emphasizes the importance of the Twenty-third Psalm with these words,

The Book of Psalms, provides much of the poetry of our religious and spiritual lives. Yet one psalm above all the others calls to us most powerfully—Psalm 23, "The LORD is my shepherd." This is the psalm that comforts us when we grieve, that offers us refuge when we are lost, and that proffers hope when we are hopeless. But why? What is it about the 23rd Psalm that makes this the hymn of solace? Let me suggest four things.

First, the psalm is compact and easily memorized: only fifty-seven words in the original Hebrew, and rarely more than twice that in the . . . English translations. Second, it speaks to us where we are, reminding us of what is available to us now in the midst of our fear, grief, and sadness. This is not a hymn to past glory or future redemption, but an invitation to walk with God here and now. Third, Psalm 23 speaks not only about God, but also to God; shifting mid-hymn from third person to second person, from "he" to "Thou," from God as idea to God as presence. And fourth, Psalm 23 asks nothing of us, but speaks instead of the unconditional grace and gifting of God's love. We don't earn God's love; we awaken to it: God is my shepherd no matter how wayward a sheep I may be. . . .

This guide is to be read and reread. It was not written for your bookshelf, but for your night-stand, purse, and

34

briefcase. . . . The psalm . . . is meant to travel with you as you walk through the shadowed valley of your own mortality, for it is only in the immediacy of your own life that the 23rd Psalm reveals the reality of God shepherding you at every turn.[11]

Dr. Robert Ketcham declared,

During nearly forty years in the pastorate I have heard hundreds of people quote the first verse of Psalm Twenty-three, when as their pastor I knew that the verse had almost no application to their daily experience. They could quote the words, "The LORD is my Shepherd, I shall not want," but I knew their life was a wilderness of "want." What these dear ones really meant was, "The Lord is my *Saviour*, and I am glad He is." They had failed utterly to realize that there is a vast difference between the *Saviourhood* of Jesus Christ and the *Shepherdhood* of Jesus Christ. One may know the Lord as *Saviour* and know almost nothing of Him as *Shepherd*, as revealed in this marvelous psalm.

Psalm Twenty-three is the highest, widest, most glorious experience into which it is possible for God to lead a born-again believer this side of Heaven.[12]

When searching for the right words for a conclusion for this chapter, I only found more truth and descriptions that defy endings. In fact the psalm begins with "The LORD," and with each phrase it gets bigger and bigger, until it merges into eternity with its last

11. Shapiro, *Guide to Psalm 23*.
12. *I Shall Not Want*, 7, 12.

words—"for ever." There is no ending! Though we will never fully describe the truths of Psalm 23, the following homespun illustration will help us get just one more glance at this great, life-changing truth that lies before us—

A former acquaintance used to enjoy telling of working on the tugboats on the mighty Mississippi River. Occasionally, the crew would run the boat ashore to a dock to take on needed supplies. While standing on the dock, he could look northward and see the next bend in the river in that direction, and then look to the south to the next bend in that direction. From the dock, although it was a beautiful sight, the only river he could see was from one bend to another. But when they pushed the tug back into the middle of the stream, continued their journey down that mighty waterway, and rounded the next bend, they saw more river. So it was with each curve of the river until they finally emerged into the Gulf of Mexico and looked out into that great body of water that was more than the eye could behold.

The obvious truth of the illustration is that rounding the bend didn't make the boat or the river any bigger, it only put the traveler in a position where he could see more of a river that had been there all the time—he got in the current of that mighty, powerful stream of flowing water, and it carried him to where he could see parts of the river he could not see from the dock.

The application, of course, is that there is a Spirit-filled, Spirit-led victorious Christian life that brings the glorious results of seeing more of Christ with each new experience in life or with each new truth learned, but this writer is convinced many Christians are on the dock looking at the beauty of the river (or maybe back at the world behind them). They may even have an enormous amount of knowledge about rivers and navigation; they maybe even write guide books, journals, and essays about rivers; or they may be in the shipbuilding business, but there is a lot of river they have never seen; nor have they ever felt the flow or force of the river.

It is beyond obvious that one could not board the tugboat with his feet and leave his hands on the dock—or send his ears and leave his eyes on the dock. Either the whole man goes, or none of him goes. It's either all or nothing, and so it is with the Christian life.

Admittedly, salvation is the beginning, but total consecration to Christ should be the goal of every believer in this life.

The Apostle Paul said it like this,

> I beseech you therefore, brethren, by the mercies of God, that ye present your bodies a living sacrifice, holy, acceptable unto God, *which is* your reasonable service. And be not conformed to this world: but be ye transformed by the renewing of your mind, that ye may prove what *is* that good, and acceptable, and perfect, will of God. (Romans 12:1–2)

Dr. Don Green, the long time pastor of Parker Memorial Baptist Church of Lansing, Michigan, is known for his prayer life and his preaching on consecration. Dr. Green's sermons are always filled with admonitions to separate from worldliness and carnality and have the power of God upon one's life, and in normal conversation he almost always poses the question, "When did you make your consecration?"

Jesus said it like this—"Whosoever he be of you that forsaketh not all that he hath, he cannot be my disciple" (Luke 14:33).

The highly respected Dr. Charles Keen of Milford, Ohio, after reviewing the book *Personal Consecration* by Hubert Brooke said, "I have never believed that discipleship was twenty pages of filling in the blanks."

Discipleship is simply the result of total consecration to Christ, and in our search for words to describe that consecration, we found, "The LORD *is* my shepherd; I shall not want," and five following verses that describe that one phrase.

In this writer's opinion, the six verses of Psalm 23 constitute the greatest document ever penned in the history of the world for the Christian.

It is our goal in the next and final part of this book to show that Psalm 23 is not just a beautiful piece of poetry; it is a description of a consecrated, living relationship between our Good Shepherd and the sheep of His pasture.

And now, with the conclusion of this overview, we direct our efforts toward the study of these six verses with the goal of helping the sheep see that *the Lord is my Shepherd, and that's enough,* and thereby, in the words of Jeremiah Burroughs, help believers to enjoy the *rare jewel of Christian contentment.*

Part Three

A Devotional Commentary on Psalm Twenty-three

My Shepherd is the Lord; I know
No care, or craving need:[1]

---

1. Rev. J. Keble, "Psalm Twenty-three in English Verse."
All subsequent quotes opposite the chapter headings are from the same.

Psalm 23:1

"The LORD is my shepherd; I shall not want"

As I have researched and studied in preparation for writing this book, many passages of Scripture that before lived in obscurity to me have now come to light. In God's own time, the truths that were there all along have now been made to live in my heart. They have given me greater love and appreciation for, and many precious hours of personal fellowship with, my Good Shepherd—the Lord Jesus Christ. The experience has been priceless!

In this brief one hundred eighteen word passage, it seems there are as many sermons as there are words, and each and every phrase could provide enough truth for its own book. For this cause there may be times that the overall continuity of the passage seems to be broken, but when we realize each and every one of the individual blessings mentioned are the result and outflow of one statement— "The LORD *is* my shepherd"—there will be perfect harmony.

And now let's begin our study with the first two words.

The LORD is translated from God's name, *Jehovah*, written in Hebrew as an unpronounceable YHWH, or YHVH.

According to a Jewish information website,

> In Jewish thought, a name is not merely an arbitrary designation, a random combination of sounds. The name conveys the nature and essence of the thing named.

41

...A name should be treated with the same respect as the thing's reputation. For this reason, God's Names, in all of their forms, are treated with enormous respect and reverence in Judaism....

Some rabbis assert that a person who pronounces YHVH according to its letters (instead of using a substitute) has no place in the World to Come, and should be put to death. Instead of pronouncing the four-letter Name, we usually substitute the Name "Adonai," or simply say "Ha-Shem," meaning "the Name."

The site also states that the orthodox Jewish scribes would not write "God" when referring to Jehovah. They rendered it "G-d".[1]

Dr. Adrian Rogers declared that so sacred was the name YHWH that Jewish priests would only pronounce it once a year in the Temple, and even then only behind the veil in the Holiest of Holies.

Dr. Rogers went on to say, "Evangelist Angel Martinez has described the LORD in this way,"

The LORD, the One who made the world and everything that is in it, the One who lit the taper of the sun and put the stars in their places. . . . The One who threw a carpet of green grass upon the earth and tacked it down with flowers, the One who scooped up the valleys and piled up the hills, the One who took the song of the seraph and robed it with feathers and gave it to the nightingale, the One who took the rainbow and wove it into a scarf

1. Tracey R. Rich, "The Name of G-d," Judaism 101, accessed August 28, 2017, http://www.jewfaq.org/name.htm.

and threw it about the shoulders of a dying storm, . . . At evening time, He pulls down the shade of the night and shoots it through with sunset fire.[2]

That great orator, Dr. R. G. Lee, once said,

For mortal man to try to explain God would be like trying to add beauty to a blushing red rose with a kindergartner's crayon, or add brightness to the sun's rays with a flashlight.

It would be more realistic to believe we could measure the amount of water in all the oceans of the world with a teaspoon, or count the grains of sand on every beach on the planet one-by-one, than to give an adequate description of JEHOVAH.

The LORD is

In a sermon he titled "The *Is*-ness of God," the preacher said, "The LORD that *is*, always has been *is*, and always will be *is*. He is not a has been; He is an *is*."

"The LORD *is*" is a statement of fact without scientific proof. An unbeliever may reject God because he can't find Him or prove that He "is" through scientific methods. One preacher rightly said that the agnostic will never find God as long as he is looking for Him in a test tube in some laboratory, or on the backside of a planet while exploring the universe in a space ship, or by peering through a telescope.

The story was told of a fool (see Psalm 14:1) standing on a soap box at a speakers' corner proclaiming to a crowd of spectators, "There

2. Angel Martinez, quoted by Adrian Rogers, *The Lord Is My Shepherd*, 15.

is no God!" Immediately, a voice came from an older gentleman on the backside of the crowd saying, "He means that he knows of."

Job gave us some insight as to why unbelievers can't find God when he said,

> Behold, I go forward, but he *is* not *there*; and backward, but I cannot perceive him: On the left hand, where he doth work, but I cannot behold *him*: **he hideth himself** on the right hand, that I cannot see *him*. (Job 23:8–9)

> When **he hideth *his* face**, who then can behold him? (Job 34:29)

We read also in Psalm 89:46, "How long, LORD? wilt thou **hide thyself** for ever?" and in Isaiah 45:15, "**Thou *art* a God that hidest thyself.**"

To paraphrase these statements we would say, "If God doesn't reveal Himself, unbelievers will never find Him," but the good news is that God has revealed Himself within the pages of His own divinely, inspired Word—

> Without faith *it is* impossible to please *him*: for **he that cometh to God must** [not prove, but] **believe that he is**, and *that* he is a rewarder of them that diligently seek him. (Hebrews 11:6)

> So then faith *cometh* by hearing, and hearing by the word of God. (Romans 10:17)

There is no other God.

We have no trouble stating emphatically that "The LORD *is*," and we can be just as dogmatic in stating that *He is the only God that there is*.

Consider these very clear and concise statements—

> We know that an idol *is* nothing in the world, and that *there is* none other God but one. (1 Corinthians 8:4)

> Is there a God beside me? yea, *there is* no God. (Isaiah 44:8)

> Paul hath persuaded and turned away much people, saying that they be no gods, which are made with hands. (Acts 19:26)

> The LORD he *is* God in heaven above, and upon the earth beneath: *there is* none else. (Deuteronomy 4:39)

> Thus saith the LORD the King of Israel, and his redeemer the LORD of hosts; I *am* the first, and I *am* the last; and beside me *there is* no God. (Isaiah 44:6)

> But to us *there is* but one God, the Father, of whom *are* all things, and we in him; and one Lord Jesus Christ, by whom *are* all things, and we by him. (1 Corinthians 8:6)

Any god other than Jehovah is only in the imagination of depraved humanity, and the many images fashioned by the hands of men are only expressions of their faulty view of God. Expressing those faulty views is strictly forbidden in the second of the Ten Commandments. (See Exodus 20:4 and Deuteronomy 5:8.)

Once while visiting a prison in Old Mexico, I was put into a cell with a new convert and told I had forty minutes to teach him a Bible lesson. Knowing people of the entire country were predominantly Roman Catholics, and all this new convert had ever known was the idol-worshipping mockery of Christianity, I had the opportunity of administering the first test of real, genuine salvation. Jesus Himself said, "He that is of God heareth God's words" (John 8:47), so we read the verse that forbids the making of graven images, and I proceeded to give several reasons why we could never make an image of the one true God. Then I concluded our study with the final statement, "You could never make an image of God, because you couldn't make it big enough." Before I left the cell, the convert marked his Bible at Exodus 20 and said, "No more images."

A nine hundred foot tall Jesus is a fake.

Several years ago when the "faith healer," Oral Roberts, claimed to have had a vision of a nine hundred foot tall Jesus, Bible-believers had no trouble rejecting Robert's vision of a fake Jesus for one simple reason—it was far too small!

Our God is a living God.

Back in 1966 William Hamilton, a professor of church history at a small divinity school in Rochester, New York, drew the attention of just about every Christian publisher and Bible preacher in the country when he made the statement, "God is dead."

[Hamilton] believed that the concept of God had run its course in human history. Civilization now operated according to secular principles. And, he said, churches should, too, by helping people learn to care for one another unconditionally, without illusions about heavenly rewards.[3]

Although God needed no defense, this writer along with many others, responded to the theology of a dead God as being no theology at all. It was simply the ramblings of an individual that was educated beyond his intelligence.

I remember one, good, Bible-believing preacher offering a rebuttal that I enjoyed that went something like this—I know God is not dead because I talked to Him just a little while ago! However, for those who entertain the thought of God dying, When did He die? Who signed His death certificate? In what obituary column did the funeral arrangements appear? Where did they bury Him? Who conducted the funeral? Who was close enough to the deceased to identify Him? And why was I not notified. I'm a member of the family?

I am reminded of another college professor, who was also educated beyond his intelligence, standing beside a farmer and his mule, trying to show him the Gospel from a Greek New Testament. After some time with no progress in sight, the farmer said to the professor, "Your problem is that you are too smart for your own good."

It has been said that an intelligent person is not always someone who knows a lot. He is a person who can tell you what he knows. Former president, Ronald Reagan, once said, "The trouble with our liberal friends is not that they are ignorant; it's just that they know so much that isn't so."

---

3. McDonald, *The Socialite Who Killed a Nazi with Her Bare Hands*, 233.

An image with cold feet

An interesting story condemning the worship of a false, dead god is the testimony of Antonio Arellano of Monterrey, Mexico. While on a mission trip to his city with a group from the United States, I asked Antonio to give his testimony to our group. He then told of being raised in a drunkard's home. Antonio said his dad would come home from work almost every day and beat his children and his wife. Antonio and his older brother, Roberto, Jr., would go to an image of the virgin Mary in their front yard and pray for a miracle, but the miracle never came.

Once a year Roberto, Sr. would take the entire family to the city for one of the "church's" celebrations, at which time they would stand in line for hours for an opportunity to kiss the foot of a crucifix. Brother Antonio said that, even as a small child, when he kissed the foot of that graven image of Jesus, he always noticed that it was cold.

Antonio went on to tell how one day, seemingly out of nowhere, a big Americana missionary rode up to his house on horseback and asked for a drink of water. Mrs. Arellano gave him a glass of water, and he then asked if he could read something to the family. Roberto, Sr. gave his approval, and the missionary opened a "black book," and after reading several verses said, "Jesus Christ is alive." Brother Antonio said when he said that, it was like an electrical shock to our hearts—we thought He was dead.

That day God saved the whole family. Out of curiosity I asked Antonio, "How long did it take for your dad to manifest a change?" Antonio said, "He changed immediately, and within thirty days he was preaching the Gospel."

The Arellano family didn't need to prove that "The LORD *is*." They just needed to believe what the missionary read from the Bible was true.

I never looked at it like that.

Another enlightening illustration of who God is and where you can find Him was given by a pastor in central Mississippi. When he made a visit to the home of Dianne, she immediately claimed to be an atheist.

After only a few minutes into the visit, the pastor mentioned God, and Dianne said, "I told you I'm an atheist."

He asked, "Dianne, do you think you know everything about everything?"

"No. No one knows everything," was her honest reply.

"Do you think you know half of everything there is to know?"

"No, I don't."

"Well, just for an illustration, let's imagine we can put all of the knowledge you have in one place and everything you don't know in another place by itself."

"Okay, all the information I know nothing about is all by itself. But what's the point?"

He then asked, "Dianne, do you think God might be in the information you know nothing about?"

She thought about it before replying, "You know, I never looked at it like that."

The pastor told her, "Dianne, you're not an atheist, you're an agnostic. The question is, are you an honest or a dishonest agnostic?

A dishonest agnostic says, 'I don't know if there is a God or not, and I'm not willing to find out,' but an honest agnostic says, 'I don't know if there is a God, but I am willing to find out.'"

"How do I do that?" she asked.

He pulled out a little booklet and handed it to her, explaining, "I'm going to leave this with you. It's the Gospel of John, and it only has twenty-one chapters. All I ask is that you read just one chapter each day, and as you read, ask yourself, 'Who does Jesus Christ claim to be, and what am I going to do about it?'"

The following Sunday Dianne was in the morning services; when the pastor gave the invitation, he saw her step out and come to the front of the church. When he asked her why she had come forward, she replied, "I want to be baptized and join this church."

"But Dianne," he said, "you have to be saved first."

With a smile, she answered, "That's already been taken care of. The Lord saved me the day after you visited my home. I never got all the way through the first chapter of that little booklet you gave me before I knew who He was and what I needed to do about it."

"The LORD *is*" declares His existence, and some people go no further than to admit Jehovah does exist, but *is* not only means "that which exists; that which is." It also means "**the *quality* of existence**."[4]

When Dianne, the professing atheist, took an honest look at the Scriptures, she not only discovered He does exist—she discovered the *quality of His existence.*

---

4. *The Oxford English Dictionary*, 2nd ed.

The phrase "The LORD *is*" is found hundreds of times in the Old Testament and at least fifty times in the Psalms, with many of His qualities following the statement. Phrases like,

> God [The Lord] *is* our refuge and strength, a **very present help in trouble.** (Psalm 46:1)

Dr. S. M. Lockridge paraphrased "a very present help in trouble" this way—"In your darkest hour He is able to get to where you are quicker than right now."

> **The LORD** *is* my rock, and my fortress, and my deliverer; my God, my strength, . . . my buckler, and the horn of my salvation, *and* my high tower. (Psalm 18:2)

> **The LORD** *is* my light and my salvation; . . . the LORD *is* the strength of my life. (Psalm 27:1)

> **The LORD** *is* my strength and my shield. (Psalm 28:7)

> **The LORD is** my defence; and my God *is* the rock of my refuge. (Psalm 94:22)

> **The LORD** *is* my strength and song, and is become my salvation. (Psalm 118:14)

The LORD *is* my shepherd.

The Nature and Spirit of the Sheep

When one says, "The LORD *is* my shepherd," they are confessing that they are the sheep of His pasture.

In order to understand the comparison God makes between His people and sheep, we need to understand some of the habits and the nature of the sheep; but first a word of caution to those who think all sheep are the same.

Never trust the ram.

The following words come from *A Beginner's Guide to Raising Sheep*—

> While sheep are generally docile, non-aggressive animals, this is not usually the case with rams, especially during the breeding season. Rams can be very aggressive and have been known to cause serious injuries, even death, to people. A ram should never be trusted, even if it is friendly or was raised as a pet. It is important to always know where the ram is and to never turn your back on him. Children should be restricted access to rams during the breeding season.
>
> . . . To discourage butting, you should avoid petting or scratching a ram on the head. Otherwise, the ram may see this as a challenge or aggressive behavior. In general, the ram sees you as part of the flock and wants to dominate you.[5]

We find this truth tucked away in the Scriptures in the statement found in Isaiah 53:7: "A sheep before **her** shearers is dumb." But when we read the same passage quoted in Acts 8:32, we find the emphasis switched from **her** to **his**: "like a lamb dumb before **his** shearer . . ." We notice that the "**his**" is a lamb and not a full grown ram. The

---

5. Susan Schoenian, "Sheep 201: Sheep Behavior," Sheep 101, accessed February 20, 2018, http://www.sheep101.info/201/behavior.html.

obvious truth is that the female sheep will offer no rebellion, but the male sheep will only submit while it is a lamb—once it becomes an adult ram, it will resist opposition and fight back.

Sheep are dumb.

In all of my research I did not find one shepherd who commended sheep for their intelligence. It was as though they all spake with one voice declaring sheep to be "dumb animals." In my effort to gain firsthand information, I made a personal visit to a sheep ranch and my suspicion was confirmed. The owner said the only thing you could train sheep to do was to recognize your voice, especially when they were called at feeding time.

Avery Rogers said,

> The sheep . . . knows only a few things by nature—it is hard to teach it anything. You have never seen a sheep in a circus, have you? I always thought a hog was the dumbest creature there was until I saw a show where they taught hogs to jump through hoops.
>
> [Sheep] know the shepherd, they know his voice and they know to follow him. That's it. . . . If you are valedictorian of your class, . . . captain of your football team, . . . if you rank high in your grades and astound everyone with your genius, you don't get very far with God [the Good Shepherd].[6]

---

6. *The Shepherd and His Sheep*, 101.

Sheep are ceremonially clean and clean by nature, but become very dirty through no fault of their own.

Sheep chew the cud and are cloven-footed making them ceremonially clean (see Leviticus 11:3), and by nature they enjoy clean places better than mud and filth like a hog. But they become very dirty if compared to animals like the cat, dog, bird, etc., which will be seen making an attempt to clean themselves; or like other animals such as the horse, donkey, cow, etc., which will naturally shed their old hair at the beginning of each new season and grow a newer, cleaner coat. But the sheep has no way of cleaning itself. If its wool becomes wet and matted with dirt, or dirty from lying where other sheep have been, the wool can produce a very offensive odor.

Some shepherds have been known to take a baby lamb and place it on the opposite side of a river from its mother so she will swim across the river to get to her lamb and be washed by the flowing water from some of her filth.

One writer during the cattle–sheep wars of the western United States wrote,

> A sheep just oozes out a stink
> That drives a cowman plumb to drink!
> Its hoofs leave flavors on the grass
> That even make the old cows pass. . . .
> Sheep ranges, cattle sure won't graze,
> But—cowboys hate sheep anyways![7]

---

7. Frank Benton, "How I Love Sheep."

Sheep are defenseless.

Part of the reason a sheep is defenseless is because of its senses. A sheep neither sees nor hears very well, partly because of the long wool which grows over its eyes and ears. But even if it could see or hear the enemy coming, it is not swift in flight. Instead of running away, it will make a feeble effort to get away and will then lie down and let whatever wild animal is there do its worst. There are other animals that are not swift in running, but they have some kind of weapon to use. A female sheep does not have claws, antlers, quills, or a dreadful aroma to fight with. In conflict they are readily overcome. Just as the child of God has no wisdom of his own, so he has no strength of his own.

Paul tells us in 2 Corinthians 3:5, "Not that we are sufficient of ourselves to think any thing as of ourselves; but our sufficiency *is* of God." He was saying that when he was strong (when he depended upon his own power) he was weak, but when he was weak (depending upon the power of the Lord) he was strong (2 Corinthians 12:10). We are weak like sheep—defenseless against Satan and the enemies of our soul. Surely we will be overcome if we are left to ourselves.

Sheep have no sense of direction.

A sheep will start nibbling the grass with its head down, and it will nibble and nibble along as it finds more and sweeter grass, without any awareness it is wandering away from the rest of the flock. Finally, when it lifts its head and finds no shepherd or other sheep in sight, it becomes confused and distressed because it hasn't a clue how to get back. If left alone, that wandering sheep will probably become entangled in thorns and give up and die.

Sheep are known to be very meek, timid, and easily disturbed.

Phillip Keller says,

> Even a stray jackrabbit suddenly bounding from behind a bush can stampede a whole flock [of sheep]. When one startled sheep runs in fright a dozen others will bolt with it in blind fear, not waiting to see what frightened them.[8]

Sheep are affectionate animals.

One writer declares that even the shepherd couldn't deal harshly, cruelly, or roughly with his sheep. The voice and dealings of the shepherd had to be tender; full of pathos and kindness. This reminds us of Matthew 11:29, where Jesus said, "Take my yoke upon you, and learn of me; for I am **meek and lowly** in heart: and ye shall find rest unto your souls." Also, in Isaiah 40:11, we read, "He shall feed his flock like a shepherd: he shall gather the lambs with his arm, and carry *them* in his bosom, *and* shall **gently** lead those that are with young."

> When the shepherd takes one of his sheep into his arms and fondles it, it responds with everything it has. Or if he becomes playful, it will frolic around him, giving little leaps of joy and wagging its tail, having the great-est time of its life. Knowing how much they need daily

8. *The Shepherd Trilogy,* 30.

affection, he will often stop during the day's journey just to spend time with them. Some sheep will step out of line and look up into its master's face with a "baaa." Calling each one by name, he will put out his hand and rub one on the head, or tickle one under the chin and speak some endearment into its ear. . . .

[Sheep] are willing to give up their wool without resistance, without bleating or fighting. They will just lie there and let you cut it off and never hate you for taking it. . . .

There is no contention or offensiveness about them. And that is to be the spirit of the saints of God. In Titus 3:2, it says, "To speak evil of no man, to be no brawlers, *but* **gentle**, shewing all **meekness** unto all men." And Ephesians 4:2–3 emphasizes the same thing: "With all lowliness and meekness, with longsuffering, forbearing one another in love; Endeavouring to keep the unity of the Spirit in the bond of peace." How hard that is for most of us. We are so strong and . . . so self-sufficient. Our rights are so important to us that we often forget that we are to be a meek people.[9]

Figuratively speaking, predators need to be "taken out," and Bible preaching must include some rebuke, reproof, and exhortation for godly living, but as already stated, sheep don't respond well to harshness. As one preacher said, "Jerking the hide off of the sheep will eliminate any hope for baby lambs or wool in the future."

---

9. Rogers, *The Shepherd and His Sheep*, 106–7.

Some preachers, trying to build a monument to themselves by *"slaying the sheep,"* are a good testimony of the mercy of God. As our good friend, the late Dr. Don Mangus, used to say, "Can you imagine how many sheep God has allowed to be slaughtered training one shepherd?"

Sheep are gregarious.

According to *A Beginners Guide to Raising Sheep,*

> Sheep are best known for their strong flocking [herding] and following instinct. They will run from what frightens them and band together in large groups for protection. This is the only protection they have from predators. There is safety in numbers. It is harder for a predator to pick a sheep out of a group than to go after a few strays.

The article goes on to say,

> Sheep are very social animals. In a grazing situation, they need to see other sheep. In fact, ensuring that sheep always have visual contact with other sheep will prevent excess stress when moving or handling them. . . . A sheep will become highly agitated if it is separated from the rest of the flock. [10]

Sheep depend heavily upon their vision.

God designed the sheep's eyes with tremendous peripheral vision so it can easily see if there are other sheep close by—

10. "Sheep 201: Behavior." *A Beginner's Guide to Raising Sheep.* Accessed January 04, 2018. http://www.sheep101.info/201/behavior.html.

Sheep have a very large pupil that is somewhat rectangular in shape. The eyeball is placed more to the side of the head, which gives sheep a much wider field of vision. With only slight head movement, sheep are able to scan their surroundings. Their field of vision ranges from 191 to 306 degrees, depending upon the amount of wool on their face.[11]

Sheep like to fellowship.

Shepherd J. Douglas MacMillan said, "It is the nature of sheep to fellowship with sheep." He goes on—

At one period . . . a white goat appeared on our hill. . . . It thought it was a sheep! But the funny thing was that not one sheep . . . believed that goat was a sheep, and they would have nothing to do with it. Why? Because sheep fellowship with sheep . . . a sheep does not like goats.[12]

Sheep are domestic animals.

Shepherding is so important that the life of the sheep depends on the faithfulness of an able shepherd.

Animals such as horses, cats, dogs, pigs, and many others may be separated from an owner and yet survive in the wild—but not a sheep. When sheep are left to themselves, they will self destruct. They may wander into the wild and with no way to protect themselves be killed by some wild beast of prey, or they may become cast, without

11. Ibid.
12. MacMillan, *The Lord Our Shepherd*, 82.

enough strength to get back up on their own. They may even destroy their own grazing land and starve to death. There must be an able shepherd that the sheep trust to lead, protect, and provide for them.

From these few temperamental traits of sheep, we can draw many analogies and illustrations of the people of God and their personal relationship to Him. We can also find in the sheep a great type of the nation of Israel, especially in their suffering.

Sheep Are a Type of Israel

The sheep have suffered.

Many times in the Old Testament, and especially in the Psalter (Israel's song book), the Israelites were compared to sheep. (See Psalm 44:11, 22; 49:14; 74:1; 78:52; 79:13.) In Psalm 95:7, we are clearly told that "he *is* our God; and we *are* the people of his pasture, and the sheep of his hand," and in Psalm 100:3, we read, "Know ye that the LORD he *is* God: *it is* he *that* hath made us, and not we ourselves; *we are* his people, and the sheep of his pasture."

In Numbers 27:16–17, Moses requested that the LORD

> set a man over the [Israelitish] congregation, Which may go out before them, and which may go in before them, and which may lead them out, and which may bring them in; that the congregation of the LORD be not **as sheep** which have no shepherd.

However, the sad truth is that many of Israel's leaders became evil, idle shepherds, and the sheep suffered and were scattered.

The trail of blood.

As you follow the trail of sheep through the centuries, you will find much hatred, torture, and slaughter of the innocent animals. Though this is a study of Psalm 23, and most of our comments about sheep are related to the land of Israel, the attitude toward sheep and shepherds has been the same all over the world. And never has that hatred been more strongly emphasized than in the early days of the settling of the Old West in America.

It is reported that right after the Civil War in 1865, there were more sheep in America than cattle, but many of the shepherds grazing their sheep on the open range allowed their sheep to stay in one place too long and much of the grazing land was destroyed. For this cause the Sheep and Cattle Wars broke out, and even into the first half of the twentieth century, thousands of sheep were shot, burned, driven over cliffs, poisoned, and clubbed to death with spokes from wagon wheels, and many shepherds were killed.

The report is that "between 1870 and 1920, approximately 120 engagements occurred in eight different states or territories. At least 54 men were killed and some 50,000 to over 100,000 sheep were slaughtered."[13]

The following reports come from *America's Sheep Trails,* an excellent source for the history of sheep and shepherds, especially in the western United States—

Nothing angered the cattle owner more than the dallying of sheep, across range which he normally used . . . .

13. "Sheep Wars," Wikipedia, December 06, 2017, accessed January 04, 2018, https://en.wikipedia.org/wiki/Sheep_Wars.

In many instances poisoned feed was thrown near the bedground so that the hungry flock would pick it up when it moved in the morning. . . . In January, 1921, west of Craig, Colorado, N. N. Chapman and Isadore Bolten decided to throw their flocks together. Bolten had just purchased sixteen to seventeen hundred ewes, while Chapman's band was another sixteen hundred head. . . . When the partners arrived to merge the flocks, they found that Chapman's herder had been forced by cattlemen to hold his band on the bedground practically a month. While it was in a half starved condition, the cowboys had thrown poisoned corn where the sheep could get it, causing the death of about three hundred head.

One of the most diabolical attacks took place near the San Francisco peaks north of Flagstaff, Arizona, in 1884. Ten bands of sheep were camped near each other in an attractive natural park when there rushed across their bedgrounds a hundred or more wild horses with long rawhides dragging from their tails. Fifteen or twenty head were wearing huge cowbells around their necks "to encourage speed." They broke out of timber with cowboys in wild pursuit, yelling and shooting. The herders met the oncoming wave with rifle shots but this merely turned the horses to milling among the defenseless flocks. Twenty-five thousand sheep were thrown into a bleating, terrified mob. Hundreds were killed and maimed, and a week was required to re-group the disordered bands.

On August 24, 1905, about 10:00 P.M., ten masked men rode into the sheep camp of Louis Gantz on Shell Creek, forty miles from Basin in the Big Horn Valley of Wyoming, and shot, dynamited, or clubbed, approximately four thousand animals. A pair of horses was also shot, the herder's and camp tender's wagons were burned, and the grain, provisions, and other camp equipment destroyed. Most brutal of all, the sheep dogs were tied to the wheels of the flaming wagons and scorched to death. . . . When the camp was destroyed, the herders were warned to leave the country and never to come back.

Some cowhands insisted that this type of attack involved too much work, so dynamite charges fitted with percussion caps were thrown into flocks feeding close together or massed in a corral.

A variation of these methods was the "rim-rocking" of a band. Taking advantage of the natural flocking instinct of sheep and their blind tendency to follow their leaders, the camp raiders would start a flock toward the edge of a cliff, shouting and shooting until the flock was in a panic. Flank riders kept the band headed for the edge, and regardless of the reaction of the leaders when they faced the cliff, the sheep pressing behind would crowd them over. Once started, the remainder of the flock stupidly followed, jumping blindly to their deaths. Since sheep naturally grazed the rougher country, it was quite easy for those attacking a camp to find a place where this procedure could be followed. Montana cattlemen crossed the Wyoming boundary in 1904 and attacked the flock of George Crosby, apparently in retaliation for his grazing south of the Pryor Mountains just over the line in Montana. About five hundred head rushed over a precipice into a deep gorge, where the animals were crushed to death.

Sometimes quicksands replaced the high cliffs. On the Little Colorado River in East Central Arizona in 1884, a party of cattlemen raided a sheep camp where two outfits were located. Well armed and well mounted, the cowboys swooped down on the surprised herders and tied them to trees. The river bottom was covered with a bottomless sand. In one great mass, four thousand head were crowded there to mire down and die.

The most cruel method of attacking sheep was by the use of fire. It was conventional to burn the camp wagons and camp equipment, regardless of whether there were hazards to occupants. But the public was revolted when in 1889, during a raid on the sheep camp of John Jost in the Elk Mountain District (Carbon County, Wyoming), a sleeping child in one of the flaming wagons was barely rescued in time. It suffered serious burns.

But setting fire to helpless sheep was even more barbarous. Early in 1887, twenty-six hundred head were burned in the corrals of Charles Herbert near Tie Siding. A few animals were killed and the fire was started. Then the sheep were crowded into the flames, igniting the wool, and the poor animals could not scatter within the confines of the corral. Most of them burned to death or were suffocated where they crowded together.[14]

The Jews have suffered.

As we compare the suffering sheep to the persecuted Jews, historical records like these remind us of Deuteronomy 28, where God declared to Israel,

And it shall come to pass, **if thou shalt hearken diligently unto the voice of the LORD thy God,** to observe *and* to do all his commandments which I command thee this day, that the LORD thy God will set thee on high above all nations of the earth: And all these blessings shall come on thee, and overtake thee, if thou shalt hearken unto the voice of the LORD thy God. . . .

But it shall come to pass, **if thou wilt not hearken unto the voice of the LORD thy God,** to observe to do all his commandments and his statutes which I command thee this day; that all these curses shall come upon thee, and overtake thee. . . .

And the LORD shall scatter thee among all people, from the one end of the earth even unto the other; and there thou shalt serve other gods, which neither thou nor thy fathers have known, *even* wood and stone. And among these nations shalt thou find no ease, neither shall

---

14. Wentworth, 522, 524–526.

> the sole of thy foot have rest: but the LORD shall give thee
> there a trembling heart, and failing of eyes, and sorrow of
> mind: And thy life shall hang in doubt before thee; and
> thou shalt fear day and night, and shalt have none assur-
> ance of thy life: In the morning thou shalt say, Would
> God it were even! and at even thou shalt say, Would God
> it were morning! for the fear of thine heart wherewith
> thou shalt fear, and for the sight of thine eyes which thou
> shalt see. (Deuteronomy 28:1–2, 15, 64–67)

Serious students of the Scriptures will be quick to proclaim that Israel as a whole throughout the Old Testament rejected the Word of God, and in the New Testament it was the Jews who cried concerning Christ, "Let him be crucified," and when Stephen preached,

> Ye stiffnecked and uncircumcised in heart and ears, ye
> do always resist the Holy Ghost: as your fathers *did*, so
> *do* ye. Which of the prophets have not your fathers per-
> secuted? and they have slain them which shewed before
> of the coming of the Just One; of whom ye have been now
> the betrayers and murderers, (Acts 7:51–52)

they killed him also.

Every mistreated, rejected, tortured, and slain innocent sheep throughout history was a picture of what Israel would suffer because of her disobedience.

Consider the following brief but accurate overview of the perse-cution of the Jews—

> From the times of the Pharaohs of Egypt to the totali-
> tarian regime of Hitler in Germany, Jews have been

mercilessly tortured and discriminated against. Their cities have been burned to the ground by various armies, their unlucky newborn sons doomed for execution at the hands of the Pharaoh, and their worship severely restricted. Their temples have been razed to the ground numerous times, and they have been expelled many times from Jerusalem. They have been mercilessly chased out of their homes during the Spanish Inquisition. All in all, the persecution of Jews was mainly spurred by religious and nationalistic sentiments, and slowly zigzagged its way in terms of severity until it reached the peak in the Holocaust.[15]

The Holocaust was the time from 1941 to 1945 when Adolf Hitler's Nazi Germany and his World War II collaborators murdered over six million European Jews, including 1.5 million Jewish children. Historians tell us that Nazi propaganda portrayed them as vermin, thus dehumanizing them in an attempt to rationalize the Nazi crimes against them.

Yes, Israel has suffered severely, and they still have the great tribulation period to face which will be far worse than any persecution they have ever experienced in the history of their nation. (See Matthew 24:21.)

Like the cattlemen trying to exterminate sheep from the face of the earth, the enemies of Israel continue their effort to annihilate

---

15. Sohaib, "A Brief Historical Survey of Jewish Persecution," Albalagh, March 25, 2008, , accessed January 04, 2018, http://www.albalagh.net/kids/history/survey_jewish_persection.shtml.

them, but these people are still with us and some glorious daybreak the eyes of their understanding will be opened and they will recognize the offspring of King David as their Good Shepherd, and the nation that has been rejected and persecuted like none other, will recognize Jesus Christ as their Messiah. Then the promise of God penned by the prophet Isaiah will be a reality—

> Rejoice ye with Jerusalem, and be glad with her, all ye that love her: rejoice for joy with her, . . . For thus saith the LORD, Behold, I will extend peace to her like a river. . . . As one whom his mother comforteth, so will I comfort you [her]; and ye [she] shall be comforted in Jerusalem. (Isaiah 66:10, 12–13)

They are going home.

The divinely inspired words of the prophet Ezekiel guarantees the end of Israel's sufferings and a grand and glorious future for them in their own land, with their own king.

> As a shepherd seeketh out his flock in the day that he is among his sheep *that are* scattered; so will I seek out my sheep, and will deliver them out of all places where they have been scattered in the cloudy and dark day. (Ezekiel 34:12)

> And I will set up one shepherd over them, and he shall feed them, *even* my servant David; he shall feed them, and he shall be their shepherd. (Ezekiel 34:23)

> And David my servant *shall be* king over them; and they all shall have one shepherd: they shall also walk in

my judgments, and observe my statutes, and do them.
(Ezekiel 37:24)

The phrase "David my servant *shall be* king over them," is declaring that David, during the coming kingdom on earth, will serve as a king over Israel, while many others will serve as kings over other nations (see Revelation 5:10), with Christ ruling as the "KING OF KINGS" (Revelation 19:16), and then "All the kings of the earth shall praise thee, O LORD, when they hear the words of thy mouth" (Psalm 138:4).

Who are the other sheep?

When Jesus said to the Jews in John 10:16, "Other sheep I have, which are not of this fold: them also I must bring, and they shall hear my voice; and there shall be one fold, *and* one shepherd," was He referring to Gentile believers that would trust Christ and be included in the Church of this New Testament age? Most commentators teach that is the primary interpretation of the "other sheep," but I think not. The only view supported by Scriptures is that "this fold" refers to the Jews who were living in Judea at that time. Jesus, being of the tribe of Judah, we are left then, with the "other sheep . . . not of this fold."

Israel was one united nation until the reign of King Rehoboam when under Jeroboam, ten tribes separated to form their own northern kingdom (see 1 Kings 12). The remaining tribes under Rehoboam became the southern kingdom of Judah. These tribes have never been reunited, but according to Ezekiel 37, where we find the vision of the valley of dry, scattered bones that will be brought back into one body (verses 1–14), the two sticks that will be put into one man's hand (verses 15–23), and the plain statements of the remaining verses, Israel will someday, and maybe soon, be regathered to her homeland—

Thus saith the Lord GOD; Behold, I will take the children of Israel from among the heathen, whither they be gone, and will gather them on every side, and bring them into their own land: And I will make them one nation in the land upon the mountains of Israel; and **one king shall be king to them all**: and they shall be no more two nations, neither shall they be divided into two kingdoms any more at all: Neither shall they defile themselves any more with their idols, nor with their detestable things, nor with any of their transgressions: but I will save them out of all their dwellingplaces, wherein they have sinned, and will cleanse them: so shall they be my people, and I will be their God. And **David my servant *shall* be king over them; and they all shall have one shepherd**: they shall also walk in my judgments, and observe my statutes, and do them. And they shall dwell in the land that I have given unto Jacob my servant, wherein your fathers have dwelt; and they shall dwell therein, *even* they, and their children, and their children's children for ever: and my servant David *shall be* their prince for ever. Moreover I will make a covenant of peace with them; it shall be an everlasting covenant with them: and I will place them, and multiply them, and will set my sanctuary in the midst of them for evermore. My tabernacle also shall be with them: yea, I will be their God, and they shall be my people. And the heathen shall know that I the LORD do sanctify Israel, when my sanctuary shall be in the midst of them for evermore. (Ezekiel 37:21–28)

When Christ said, "There shall be one fold, and one shepherd," He was confirming the words of Ezekiel's prophecy, and the Apostle Paul put this truth in a more condensed form when he wrote, "And so **all** Israel shall be saved: as it is written, There shall come out of Sion the Deliverer, and shall turn away ungodliness from Jacob" (Romans 11:26).

The *all* in the previous verse is not a promise that each and every Israelite will be saved. It is a promise that the entire nation will be brought back together and as one nation have its eyes of understanding opened and recognize Christ as its Redeemer. To further strengthen this interpretation, I appeal to the words "the Deliverer, . . . shall turn away ungodliness from **Jacob**," him being the father of the twelve sons who became the twelve tribes—not just some of them, *all* of them.

Jerusalem is the capital.

The most recent, and very significant indication that Israel will soon see her King is in the announcement by President Donald Trump, on Wednesday, December 6, 2017, that the United States embassy will be moved from Tel Aviv to Jerusalem and the United States will now recognize Jerusalem as the capitol of Israel, a very necessary move since David cannot reign over the nation of Israel from Tel Aviv.

The Jacob sheep

Another incident that may or may not have to do with some part of Israel's home going, but is of interest, is with the "Jacob sheep." Although sheep have always existed in Israel, according to a report from *The Times of Israel*, a breed called the "Jacob sheep" are back in their homeland for the first time in 5,000 years.

One hundred nineteen heritage sheep, which trace their lineage back 5,000 years to the Middle East, began arriving in Israel on November 30, [2016]. It is the first time that the breed, called Jacob's sheep, has been represented in Israel since biblical times.

The breed received the name "Jacob sheep" based on Genesis chapter 30, where Jacob talks about leaving his father-in-law Laban's home and taking part of the flock as his payment for years of service. "I will pass through all thy flock to day, removing from thence all the speckled and spotted cattle, and all the brown cattle among the sheep, and the spotted and speckled among the goats: and *of such* shall be my hire ... [Genesis 30:32, 35].

The path of the breed mirrors the path of Jacob to Canaan and then Egypt. While the Jews were in Egypt, the sheep were incorporated into the North African flocks. Somewhere along the way, although the Jews returned to Israel, the uniquely speckled sheep did not return with them. [The report is that] the sheep have not been found in Israel for thousands of years.[16]

16. Melanie Lidman, "Biblical sheep in Israel for first time in millennia," *The*

Are Gentiles included?

Some teach the nation of Israel was replaced by the Church, which is a gross misinterpretation of Scripture. Nonetheless, as we have stated earlier, we do recognize Psalm 23 as part of Israel's hymn book written by David, a Jewish shepherd who became a king and died at Jerusalem, but will still in the future reign upon the earth. The parallel, of course, is Jesus Christ, a Jew who declared Himself to be the Shepherd, died at Jerusalem, and who will some day reign as the King upon this earth.

We need to remind ourselves that beginning with Genesis 12, the bulk of the Old Testament is dealing with the formation, history, and prophecy of one nation of people—the Jews. Under the inspiration of almighty God, they produced the written Word of God—the Bible, and through their lineage also came the Living Word—Jesus Christ.

But how do the Gentiles get in?

Romans 11:8, tells us that "God hath given them [the Israelites] the spirit of slumber, eyes that they should not see, and ears that they should not hear." Verse 11 says, "I say then, Have they stumbled that they should fall? God forbid: but *rather* through their fall salvation *is come* unto the Gentiles." According to verses 12 and 17, the fall of them is the riches of the world, and we being from a wild olive tree "wert graffed in among them, and with them partakest of the root and fatness of the olive tree." So when David wrote, "The LORD *is* my shepherd" in Psalm 23 (according to this passage in Romans),

---

Times of Israel, December 6, 2016, accessed September 20, 2017, http://www.timesofisrael.com/biblical-sheep-in-israel-for-first-time-in-millennia/.

since I have been "graffed in among them" and "with them" made a partaker, I too can say "The LORD *is* my shepherd" and claim all the blessing promised in Psalm 23.

The Shepherd

There is the Chief Shepherd, and there are undershepherds.

In the overview of this psalm, we made mention of three titles given to Christ. He is called the Good Shepherd, that Great Shepherd, and the Chief Shepherd, with the Chief Shepherd identified in 1 Peter 5—

> The elders which are among you I exhort, who am also an elder, and a witness of the sufferings of Christ, and also a partaker of the glory that shall be revealed: Feed the flock of God which is among you, taking the oversight *thereof,* not by constraint, but willingly; not for filthy lucre, but of a ready mind; Neither as being lords over *God's* heritage, but being ensamples to the flock. And when the **chief Shepherd** shall appear, ye shall receive a crown of glory that fadeth not away. (1 Peter 5:1–4)

Those encouraging words describe what the *Chief Shepherd* will do for His *undershepherds* when He appears in the future, but an illustration of the *Chief Shepherd* in ancient Israel will describe the ministry of a *Chief Shepherd* during this Church age.

In the vast flocks that wander over the pastoral regions of the East, consisting sometimes of five, ten, or twenty thousand sheep and goats, and scattered over a considerable tract of country, the eye and the vigilance of the owner is obviously quite inadequate to the task of overseeing and protecting so immense a charge. The duty is subdivided among a great many shepherds, to each of whom is assigned a certain proportion of the flock, which he tends,—leads to fresh pastures as the old ones are exhausted,—defends from the attacks of ravenous beasts,—takes care to have the young and the feeble tenderly conveyed from place to place,—and, in short, performs all the ordinary duties that belong to a shepherd. But as, whereever a considerable number of servants are employed, there will always be some of them careless, indolent, and ill behaved, so in order to keep so large a band of shepherds right, active, and regularly at their post, it was, and still is, customary in the East to have a chief shepherd, one set over all, who acts as general superintendent, and who is qualified for his office not only by superior authority and station, but by his eminent skill and experience in pasture, in the state and prognostics of the weather, in the diseases of sheep, and in everything relating to the proper management of a flock. This person is clothed with absolute control over the whole flocks and their keepers. To him the common shepherds must make, from time to time, their report of the health of their bleating charges, and the good or bad condition of the pasturage. It is his duty to ride through each separate division of the tribe,—to inspect the cattle,—to inquire into the character and conduct of the men under his charge; and according as he finds them active or negligent, faithful or unqualified for their situation, to reprove or dismiss the old, and appoint new ones at pleasure. From his verdict there is no appeal, and when he goes his periodical rounds, each subordinate shepherd expects to receive censure or commendation, according as it shall seem proper to his chief shepherd.[17]

The pastor is an undershepherd.

In commenting on this custom of chief shepherds and undershepherds, Dr. Avery Rogers had this to say—

Christ has some other shepherds. The word "pastor" in the Bible simply means a shepherd. But he is an undershepherd—not the chief one. He is under the authority of the Chief Shepherd. Just as in the Holy Land the chief shepherd gave orders to all the other shepherds and they all obeyed him, so the Chief Shepherd directs His undershepherds and they are to obey His authority. Now, that chief shepherd never gave his orders to the sheep. . . . He gave his orders to other shepherds.

No shepherd ever asked the sheep to vote. Wouldn't it be something if the shepherd got up one morning, called out his hundred sheep . . . and said, "All right, sheep, over there is some good water, but the grass is not so good. On

17. Jamieson, *Eastern Manners*, 435-436.

the other hand, that way has good grass, but not much water. I'm going to let you make up your mind which way you want to go. . . . Of course he wouldn't do that. No, he knew where he was going and just headed out in that direction with his sheep. In much the same way, the Chief Shepherd gives His orders to His undershepherds; they obey and lead the sheep in the ways He has told them.[18]

One will notice the chief shepherd, when surveying the various shepherds and their flocks, didn't blame the sheep for any weaknesses they might have; he laid the responsibility at the feet of the shepherd (pastor), and when applied to our day when much preaching is done with political correctness, puff talk, circular reasoning, and in generalities rather than specifics, it is no wonder many sheep (Christians) are showing severe spiritual health problems.

Shepherds who refuse to feed the sheep are described for us in Zechariah 11 and Ezekiel 34:2—

Son of man, prophesy against the shepherds of Israel, prophesy, and say unto them, Thus saith the Lord GOD unto the shepherds; Woe be to the shepherds of Israel that do feed themselves! should not the shepherds feed the flocks?

---

18. *The Shepherd and His Sheep*, 8.

A contrast that is beyond comprehension— the Lofty One becomes the Lowly One.

When we look in the Old Testament for direction in the lives of sheep and shepherds, we find the very first shepherd in Genesis 4:2: "Abel was a keeper of sheep." The story goes on to tell how Abel and his brother Cain both brought offerings to the LORD; the LORD had respect unto Abel and unto his offering, but rejected Cain's offering. Cain was very wroth, and his countenance fell. In verse 8 we read, "And Cain talked with Abel his brother: and it came to pass, when they were in the field, that Cain rose up against Abel his brother, and slew him."

Could it be that Abel loved his brother, being *one of his own*, and in the field he encouraged him to do the right thing and bring the right sacrifice, but Cain was wroth and received him not, but rather rose up against him and killed his own brother?

There may be some speculation as to the very details of the incident, but it does provide a crystal clear type of another Shepherd— the Lord Jesus Christ, who four thousand years later "**came unto His own**, and **His own received Him not**" (John 1:11), but rather cried, "Let him be crucified . . . let him be crucified" (Matthew 27:22–23).

The scenario with Cain and Abel provides us with another truth drawn from the oft used "first mention principle." The first shepherd in the Bible was hated and rejected, setting a precedent for shepherds throughout history. In Genesis 46:34, we read, "For every shepherd *is* an abomination unto the Egyptians."

Shepherding was a very menial task.

The youngest son in the family was usually the one appointed to the task of watching over the sheep, as was seen with David the youngest son of Jesse (1 Samuel 16:11). If there was no available son, then a daughter would be made a shepherdess, as with Rachel, the youngest daughter of Laban (Genesis 29:9), and Jethro's daughters who looked after the sheep (Exodus 2:16). One reason family members (son or daughter) took care of the sheep, especially in wolf country, was because a hireling was never trusted with sheep in wolf territory: "The hireling fleeth, because he is an hireling, and careth not for the sheep" (John 10:13).

Another reason the youngest son or a daughter watched over the sheep was because minding sheep was a very insignificant, humble, and undesirable task. Stalwart men of renown were not standing in line waiting for the opportunity to mind some sheep. That obvious truth sheds some light on Eve's attitude toward her two sons. When Cain was born Eve said, "I have gotten a man from the LORD," but when Abel was born not one word of praise or gratitude was recorded, and when he grew up all that is said about him was that "Abel was a keeper of sheep" (Genesis 4:1–2).

Yet another Old Testament illustration of the lowly lifestyle of a shepherd is found in 2 Samuel 7:8, where God declares that He took David from "following the sheep." The phrase is repeated in 1 Chronicles 17:7, but no reason is given for a shepherd who leads the sheep to be *following the sheep*. However, we read in Psalm 78:70–71 that God "chose David also his servant, and took him from the sheepfolds: From **following the ewes great with young.**" What a

79

job description! Following pregnant sheep around all day probably would not go for much on a resumé when applying for a better job.

One writer proclaims that

> In the days of the Prophets, sheep-herders symbolized judgment and social desolation. Dr. Joachim Jeremias says shepherds were "despised in everyday life." In general, they were considered second-class and untrustworthy.
>
> Some shepherds earned their poor reputations, but others became victims of a cruel stereotype. The religious leaders maligned the shepherd's good name; rabbis banned pasturing sheep and goats in Israel, except on desert plains.
>
> The Mishnah, Judaism's written record of the oral law, also reflects this prejudice, referring to shepherds in belittling terms. One passage describes them as "incompetent"; another says no one should ever feel obligated to rescue a shepherd who has fallen into a pit.
>
> Jeremias documents the fact that shepherds were deprived of all civil rights. They could not fulfill judicial offices or be admitted in court as witnesses.
>
> He wrote, "To buy wool, milk, or a kid from a shepherd was forbidden on the assumption that it would be stolen property."
>
> Smug religious leaders maintained a strict caste system at the expense of shepherds and other common folk.

Shepherds were officially labeled "sinners"—a technical term for a class of despised people.[19]

Jesus came down.

It was into this environment toward shepherds that Jesus came forth and made the announcement, "I am the good shepherd" (John 10:11, 14). No doubt those Jews to whom He spake remembered that the Twenty-third Psalm in their Psalter declared "The LORD" to be their Shepherd; therefore, in verse 33 they accused Jesus of blasphemy because, "that thou, being a man, makest thyself God," and they took up stones to stone Him.

When Jesus came into this world, He knew full well that He was Jehovah God in the flesh and was well aware of the sufferings He would go through to provide redemption for mankind.

Many of the prophecies of the Old Testament pointed toward the suffering Saviour, and Jesus knew all of them. Notice the words of Psalm 40:7—"Then said I, Lo, I come: in the volume of the book *it is* written of me." Who could possibly come in the volume of the book? The writer of Hebrews answered that mystery by quoting that same passage and ascribing it to none other than the Good Shepherd, the Lord Jesus Christ. (See Hebrews 10:4–10.)

In an earlier chapter we referred to Psalm 22 as a preview of Calvary. Another classic chapter with much detail foretelling the sufferings of Christ is Isaiah 53—

Who hath believed our report? and to whom is the arm of the LORD revealed? For he shall grow up before

19. Alcorn, "Shepherd Status," 85–89.

him as a tender plant, and as a root out of a dry ground: he hath no form nor comeliness; and when we shall see him, *there is* no beauty that we should desire him. He is despised and rejected of men; a man of sorrows, and acquainted with grief: and we hid as it were *our* faces from him; he was despised, and we esteemed him not. Surely he hath borne our griefs, and carried our sorrows: yet we did esteem him stricken, smitten of God, and afflicted. But he *was* wounded for our transgressions, *he was* bruised for our iniquities: the chastisement of our peace *was* upon him; and with his stripes we are healed. All we like sheep have gone astray; we have turned every one to his own way; and the LORD hath laid on him the iniquity of us all. He was oppressed, and he was afflicted, yet he opened not his mouth: he is brought as a lamb to the slaughter, and as a sheep before her shearers is dumb, so he openeth not his mouth. He was taken from prison and from judgment: and who shall declare his genera-tion? for he was cut off out of the land of the living: for the transgression of my people was he stricken. And he made his grave with the wicked, and with the rich in his death; because he had done no violence, neither *was any* deceit in his mouth. Yet it pleased the LORD to bruise him; he hath put *him* to grief: when thou shalt make his soul an offering for sin, he shall see *his* seed, he shall pro-long *his* days, and the pleasure of the LORD shall prosper in his hand. He shall see of the travail of his soul, *and*

82

shall be satisfied: by his knowledge shall my righteous servant justify many; for he shall bear their iniquities. Therefore will I divide him *a portion* with the great, and he shall divide the spoil with the strong; because he hath poured out his soul unto death: and he was numbered with the transgressors; and he bare the sin of many, and made intercession for the transgressors.

Born in Bethlehem

Even the location of Christ's birth and ministry on earth is a reflection of His ministry as a lowly shepherd. Bethlehem was not a booming metropolis. It was called "little among the thousands" (Micah 5:2), yet the Bible records two very distinct shepherds born there who would eventually serve as kings over Israel and both would die at Jerusalem. David, the one who wrote the Twenty-third Psalm, and Jesus, the One the Twenty-third Psalm is about.

Brought up in Nazareth

Other than the few short years when Jesus was taken as a young child into Egypt by Joseph and His mother to escape the murderous plan of King Herod, Jesus grew up in Nazareth, and Dr. Phillip Keller had this to say about Jesus' hometown,

If ever there was a town in the hills of Galilee greedy for gain, it was Nazareth. It was to Galilee what Las Vegas [or Bourbon Street in New Orleans, called by some "Sodom by the sea"] is to the USA or Havanah is to Cuba.

Nazareth was where the fierce passions of foreign traders crossed with the deceitfulness of crafty merchants.

It was a town notorious for its pimps, prostitutes, and evils of a hundred sorts. Here were imported all the lewd practices of Phoenicia, Persia, Rome, and the pagan tribes of Palestine.

Amid such sordid surroundings, this veritable wasteland of wickedness, the Lamb of God left His first footprints in the dust of time.

His contemporaries had no special respect for this "suffering servant" who toiled at His common trade among them. But God did. He saw Him as His only begotten Son, the first among many brethren.[20]

This description of Nazareth by Keller sheds a lot of light on the attitude of Nathanael toward that cesspool of iniquity—

Philip findeth Nathanael, and saith unto him, We have found him, of whom Moses in the law, and the prophets, did write, **Jesus of Nazareth**, the son of Joseph. And Nathanael said unto him, **Can there any good thing come out of Nazareth**? (John 1:45–46)

Of course, we who know the full story can say, "Yes, the greatest man that ever lived came out of Nazareth!"

Keller had this to say about the everyday life of Jesus—

The days of His youth and early manhood were busy with boyhood exploits and the usual achievements of human adolescence. He was not a difficult teenager,

20. *The Shepherd Trilogy*, 384.

given to tantrums and sullenness. Rather, He honoured His lowly, peasant parents taking on the trade of a simple, small-town carpenter.

Working with wood; sawing planks; shaping slabs of timber; smoothing yokes; building boxes; making plows; hammering spikes and chopping chunks of tough olive wood, or handling heavy acacia were part and parcel of His earthly drama and youthful days.

The pungent aroma of fresh cedar sawdust, the smooth feel of oak shavings curling over His big brown hands, the beautiful grain of freshly smoothed wood were the greater portion of His few short years, so simply spent in the carpenter shop.

Though He was the Lamb of God, the Everlasting One, His neighbours were the rough-and-tumble tradesmen of Nazareth, a tough, trading town. It stood on the cross-roads of commerce that criss-crossed the country. Here shepherds and farmers and camel drivers and common city people came to Christ, not to have their souls and spirits mended but broken beds and worn-out ploughs and cracked yokes.

He knew all about making candlesticks and ox stalls and shepherd crooks and farmer's forks. He was God, very God, in close touch with man, very man. Out of all these personal, private contacts came the great parables, the timeless truths, the pungent, powerful teaching of His later public ministry.

Then one day the whole scene changed. He set down His saw; hung up His hammer; put the plane on its shelf; dusted off the sawdust from His hands, and headed for the distant Jordan River.

As He moved down the slopes leading to the water's edge where John, the flaming desert firebrand, stood shouting to the masses around him, Jesus was noticed. For the first time in almost thirty years of quiet obscurity, His true identity was recognized. John, the most powerful prophet ever to appear in Israel, shouted aloud for all to hear and see—"Behold the Lamb of God!" (John 1:29).[21]

The Scriptures are very meagre in their record of these early years of our Lord's life. But in the brief and abrupt statements that are made there is a precise endorsement of the ancient prophet's pronouncement. He, the Lamb of God, would and did grow up in favour both with God and man. He matured in both wisdom and stature. His teenage years and adolescence were not marred—not marked by hostility, arrogance or tempestuous rebellion. He was a well adjusted youth.

Yet, in spite of all this, His contemporaries saw nothing of unusual or special significance in Jesus the carpenter, son of Joseph. His fellow townsmen from Nazareth looked upon Him as one of their excellent craftsmen. He learned His trade well from Joseph. He did careful,

---

21. Ibid., 376–377.

meticulous work, with skill and expertise of the highest calibre. Any yoke He made or chest He built was bound to wear well and last for years.

In the process of time, He came to be well known as the carpenter's son. He was commonly called son of Joseph. He was considered, after His father's untimely death, as "the carpenter." If one wanted first-class workmanship at fair prices, delivered on time, done with dignity, Jesus was the "man" to do it.[22]

Capernaum

When our Good Shepherd reached the age of thirty and left the carpenter shop to be baptized by John, He moved to Capernaum, which historians tells us was a large, Galilean fishing village and a very busy trading center. But our Lord never moved to Capernaum for its monetary or commercial opportunities. He went there

> that it might be fulfilled which was spoken by Esaias
> the prophet, saying, The land of Zabulon, and the land
> of Nephthalim, *by* the way of the sea, beyond Jordan,
> Galilee of the Gentiles; The people which sat in darkness
> saw great light; and to them which sat in the region and
> shadow of death light is sprung up. (Matthew 4:14–16)

We gather from these words that Capernaum was all wrapped up with this world's goods. Spiritual blindness kept them from recognizing who the preacher calling for their repentance really was.

---

22. Ibid., 383–384.

Jesus did more miracles in Capernaum than in any other place, but for the most part He was rejected there also, and with the rejection of Jesus Christ came very severe judgment. Jesus said,

> And thou, Capernaum, which art exalted unto heaven, shalt be brought down to hell: for if the mighty works, which have been done in thee, had been done in Sodom, it would have remained until this day. But I say unto you, That it shall be more tolerable for the land of Sodom in the day of judgment, than for thee. (Matthew 11:23–24)

If there happens to be a reader who doubts the severity of the judgment pronounced by Jesus on Capernaum, check her condition today, and all you will find are the ruins of what that city used to be.

Jerusalem

As the public ministry of Jesus came to a close, He made His way to Jerusalem where He would finish the work He came to do, and that was to give His life for the sheep.

> The death our Lord died was one of enormous depravity and indignity. It was part of the appalling humiliation to which He had subjected Himself from the time of His entry into our human form.
>
> From the crude, filthy manger to the cruel, ignominious cross, God in Christ had descended to the lowest depths to become identified with the lowest dregs of humanity. Many people are not prepared to face the appalling abuse heaped upon this One by ... His human contemporaries. They try, instead, to draw a deceptive

veil of respectability over the record of man's violent treatment of God.

In some cases cranks and cynics even portray Him as an imposter; pretender; a charlatan who contrived His own crucifixion. All of which only proves the point even more dramatically of man's perversion and wickedness.

When He was betrayed by one of His closest friends and companions for thirty pieces of silver, He had been sold for the literal price of a slave. Thirty shekels was the going price for a scrawny, black prisoner dragged to Jerusalem across the desert wastes from the Sudan, Ethiopia or East Africa. These wretched, weary, heartbroken fragments of the human family who had fallen into the terrible clutches of the slave traders were bartered away for thirty pieces of the bright metal. They were among the most forlorn of the earth's entire human community. Yet God in Christ reached down to their level.[23]

In considering the sovereign Creator and Ruler of this vast, indescribable universe becoming a lowly shepherd, and suffering, bleeding, and choosing to die at the hands of depraved humanity for a bunch of "sheep," 1 Timothy 3:16 aptly describes it as "the **mystery** of godliness." Some may look at a "*mystery*" as something that cannot be known, but *Strong's Concordance* defines a mystery as "the secret counsels which govern God in dealing with the righteous, which are hidden from ungodly and wicked men but plain to the godly" (*Strong's*, #3466). The *Oxford English Dictionary* defines it

23. Ibid., 395–396.

as, "A religious truth known only from divine revelation; usually, a doctrine of the faith involving difficulties which human reason is incapable of solving."

The bottom line is God had a plan, and He let us who believe on Him in on that plan. However, this family secret is far bigger than my finite mind can contain. There may be some readers with the mental capacity of a savant—there is an actual report of a savant who could "read both pages of an open book at once," one with each eye, and "retain 98% of the information he read"[24]—but I must admit I am on one page or the other, but never both at the same time. I am either thinking of the splendor of the LORD or the sufferings of our Good Shepherd, but never both in the same thought.

At this point I feel like the good, old preacher of the past who, when trying to describe some grand and glorious truth, said he felt like a squirrel in a hollow log trying to stick his head out of both ends at the same time.

Lofty and lowly—both are true.

Dr. Ketcham described the contrast between the Sovereign and the Shepherd in these words—

> This intimate association of Himself with us . . . is beautifully set before us in Psalm 147:3, 4. "He healeth the broken in heart, and bindeth up their wounds. He telleth the number of the stars; **he calleth them all by** *their*

---

24. Brogaard, Berit. "Kim Peek, the Real Rain Man." *Psychology Today*. December 11, 2012. Accessed February 22, 2018. https://www.psychologytoday.com/blog/the-superhuman-mind/201212/kim-peek-the-real-rain-man.

names." Two more widely separated spheres could hardly be imagined—*shining heavenly stars and broken human hearts!* In the one, we are taken on an excursion through the starry heavens. We are called upon to take note of the uncountable millions of celestial bodies reaching out into uncountable billions of miles in space, and there we are introduced to a Being who knows their exact number and the name of every one of them. We quail before such a Being. We fall upon our faces in fear and terror as we glimpse the majestic presence of the *God of Stars.*

The contrasting sphere is that of broken human hearts. It is as though the floor of Heaven had suddenly opened and dropped us down to earth but not into the homes and halls of earth where mirth and happiness reign. We crash on down through all of that into the very depths of human experience where broken hearts and blasted lives lie all around us. And here in this realm, too, strangely enough, we find God at work. Not now making and naming a few new stars, the greatness of which *drives us from Him in awful fear,* but healing and comforting broken hearts and binding up their wounds with a tenderness that *draws us to Him* and causes us to pillow our head upon His breast while with His own nail-pierced hand of love, He wipes every tear from our eyes.

In our experiences of sorrow, we are apt to feel that God is so far away, that He is so busy numbering and naming stars and manipulating His vast universe that He has no time to hear our feeble gasp, as with uncontrollable sorrow we turn our tear-stained faces to the sky, begging for some relief for our aching hearts. What God would have us to know from these verses is that God is never so busy manipulating the universe as vast and intricate as it is, that He does not have time to come into our little home and stand with us at the bedside of a loved one fast slipping away, and to travel with us to the little city of the dead to sustain us at the open gravesides; then to return with us to our homes and walk with us in all our ways, drying our tears, healing our hurts, and sanctifying to us our sorrows.

It was such a God who left His stars to come to the side of a broken-hearted Hagar when she cried over the imminent death of her only son. It was such a God who came to the desolate little home in Moab, where sat a broken-hearted Naomi, thinking of the three graves which contained the bodies of husband and two sons, and whispered in her ear words of hope and blessing and restoration back in the homeland of Bethlehem-Judah. It was such a God who could leave His complex universe and stand at the sealed tomb of Lazarus and weep, and in the next moment open the tomb and bring forth Lazarus. It is this God in the person of Christ who is waiting today to walk straight into the very heart of your sorrow and heal it by the touch of His nail-pierced hand. The LORD is my shepherd.[25]

The Good Shepherd cares for the sheep.

The Apostle Paul, when considering how much Christ suffered for us, concluded that He would also freely meet every need we might have—"He that spared not his own Son, but delivered him up for us all, how shall he not with him also freely give us all things?" (Romans 8:32).

Our Good Shepherd knows the needs of each and every one of His sheep. He also knows their inability to meet those needs, so He takes full responsibility for every sheep in His flock, and for His name's sake He provides, protects, guides, guards, and gives more than enough.

When Jesus made the announcement "I am the good shepherd: the good shepherd giveth his life for the sheep" (John 10:11), several verses later He also said, "I give unto them eternal life; and they shall never perish" (John 10:28). Eternal life is the kind of life God has, and that brings us back to another one of those incomprehensible, indescribable truths we believe and rejoice in knowing—that we shall understand it better by and by.

It must be a very agonizing, unsettled life when one is so filled with that old, carnal, Armenian mindset that in essence says, "Me and God make a good team. With a whole lot of me and a little bit of Him, I'll make it through!" But oh, the joy that comes to the believer's

---

25. *I Shall Not Want*, 38–39.

heart in knowing our future doesn't depend on our trying, but in the words of that great old hymn,

> And the transaction so quickly was made,
> When as a sinner I came,
> Took of the offer, of grace He did proffer;
> He saved me, O praise His dear name!

> Now I've a hope that will surely endure
> After the passing of time;
> I have a future in heaven for sure,
> There in those mansions sublime.

> And it's because of that wonderful day,
> When at the cross I believed;
> Riches eternal and blessings supernal,
> From His precious hand I received.[26]

No tolerance with God

Our Shepherd doesn't allow any tolerance or room for waste. In every phase of our lives, we come up short in some respect. Our crops never produce one hundred percent. There will always be some vegetables or plants from our garden destroyed by disease, varmints, insects, drought, etc.

The carpenter may cut the board too short, bend the nail, or lose a tool. The banker will loan money to one that will never repay. The merchant, regardless of how many safety measures he takes, will

26. John W. Peterson, "Heaven Came Down," stanzas 2b & 3

suffer some loss to thieves, and the employer will have some employees who are habitual latecomers or slothful in their work and so don't earn their pay.

There are some who realize a little loss is inevitable so they govern their loss or choose the lesser of two evils. I once encountered a cattle rancher in east Texas who was upset that someone had killed a coyote since he believed coyotes were beneficial because they always killed the weaker calves, and that minor loss would ultimately help build a stronger herd of cattle.

Some shepherds have even reported the benefits of a "sacrificial lamb." Their idea is the weakest lamb in the flock knows by instinct, and all the rest of the flock including the shepherd know, it is better for a weaker lamb to die than for a good, healthy lamb to be sacrificed to the predators. So, the lamb that is chosen to die for all the others will by instinct separate itself from the rest of the flock becoming easy prey for the hungry wolf, and while the predators are feasting on the "sacrificial lamb" the shepherd will move the rest of the flock to safety.

As we study the Old Testament, we notice that sheep were sacrificed for the shepherd, but in the New Testament there came a reversal of that order, and the Shepherd was sacrificed for the sheep. And it was not so the strong ones could live—there were no strong ones! Remember the previously quoted verse—"For when **we were yet without strength**, in due time Christ died for the ungodly" (Romans 5:6). He was the strong One!

In one year alone, according to a report for the western United States by the United States Department of Agriculture, 728,000 lambs and 229,000 adult sheep were killed by coyotes. Not a very good report!

Now let us check the success rate of our Good Shepherd, the Lord Jesus Christ—

> **All** that the Father giveth me shall come to me; and him that cometh to me I will in no wise cast out. For I came down from heaven, not to do mine own will, but the will of him that sent me. And this is the Father's will which hath sent me, that of **all** which he hath given me **I should lose nothing**, but should raise it up again at the last day. (John 6:37–39)

Since this study is about Psalm 23, written by that humble, little shepherd boy, David, we take him as a type of Christ watching over a flock of sheep. When we look at his life, we find a dead bear, a dead lion, and a dead giant, but not one lost sheep.

The 50%, 10%, and 1% parable

In the very familiar three part parable in Luke 15, we read of a father who had two sons. One of these sons was lost but eventually returned to the father's house. If that son had not of come home, the father would have suffered a 50% loss.

Then there was a woman who had ten coins and lost one of them. So, she lit a candle, swept the house, and searched diligently until she found the lost coin. If she had not found the coin, she would have suffered a 10% loss.

Finally, in the case of the shepherd with one hundred sheep, where one got lost in the wilderness, if it had not of been brought in, he would have suffered only a 1% loss.

Can the reader imagine with me that shepherd coming in from the grazing land with a flock of well-fed and watered sheep ready for a good night's rest? When the shepherd neared the public sheepfold, he stepped aside as the sheep formed themselves into a single line to pass through the narrow door. As each sheep passed by, the shepherd gently tapped it on its back with his rod and counted them one by one—1, 2, 3, ... 10, ... 50, ... 75, ... 90, ... 95, 96, 97, 98, 99, and ... that was all. There was one sheep missing!

At that point the shepherd could have taken a closer inventory to see whether it was worth going after or not. It could have been a troublemaker that was more trouble than it was worth and needed to be taken out of the flock. Or, it could have been a sick weakling that couldn't keep up or a wanderer that had a habit of straying from the flock—the Scripture doesn't give us any information about the condition of the sheep; we are only told,

> What man of you, having an hundred sheep, if he lose one of them, doth not leave the ninety and nine in the wilderness, and go after that which is lost, until he find it? (Luke 15:4)

Elizabeth C. Clephane surely knew something of the great truth—the shepherd cares for His sheep—when she wrote, "The Ninety and Nine." It was in the year 1874 that Ira Sankey found the words to her poem in a Scottish newspaper. He wrote the music for it and sang it all over England and America in his crusades with D. L. Moody.[27]

There were ninety and nine that safely lay
In the shelter of the fold.
But one was out on the hills away,
Far off from the gates of gold.
Away on the mountains wild and bare.
Away from the tender Shepherd's care.

"Lord, Thou hast here Thy ninety and nine;
Are they not enough for Thee?"
But the Shepherd made answer: "This of Mine
Has wandered away from Me;
And although the road be rough and steep,
I go to the desert to find My sheep."

But none of the ransomed ever knew
How deep were the waters crossed;
Nor how dark was the night the Lord passed through
Ere He found His sheep that was lost.
Out in the desert He heard its cry,
Sick and helpless and ready to die;

"Lord, whence are those blood drops all the way
That mark out the mountain's track?"
"They were shed for one who had gone astray
Ere the Shepherd could bring him back."

27. Sankey, *My Life Story*, 197–203.

"Lord, whence are Thy hands so rent and torn?"
"They are pierced tonight by many a thorn;"

And all through the mountains, thunder-riv'n
And up from the rocky steep,
There arose a glad cry to the gate of Heaven,
"Rejoice! I have found My sheep!"
And the angels echoed around the throne,
"Rejoice, for the Lord brings back His own!"

When the shepherd went to rescue this sheep, all it had done was get itself lost in the wilderness. In fact, a careful reading of Psalm 23 will show that none of the sheep did anything to deserve any of the blessings of the shepherd; they just enjoyed them.

A good Bible teacher in my home church illustrated the attitude of so many who treat God like a lucky-charm, a horseshoe over the door, or a rabbit's foot on a key chain that you can rub to get help in an emergency. The teacher told how before he really understood much about the Christian life and had consecrated his entire life to Christ, every time he got into some difficult situation he couldn't get himself out of, he would pray and ask God to get him through, with the idea that just as soon as the problem was solved he would take it from there.

None of us on this side of eternity can even begin to comprehend all that is included in those five little words—"The LORD *is* my shepherd," but some seem to treat that statement with the attitude that being a good shepherd and watching over the sheep is simply a guarantee that God is available at all times, so if we ever get into trouble, God will be there to help us out.

We will cover this truth in more detail when we get to verse six, but for now we borrow the words "Surely goodness and mercy shall follow me all the days of my life:" and all the days include each and every day, not just the days when trouble comes.

When we look at all the wonderful things a good shepherd did in ancient Israel to take care of his sheep (including going through whatever was necessary to get to a wandering sheep), we rejoice and try to make a lot of comparisons between those shepherds and our Good Shepherd, Christ Jesus our Lord. But in reality the comparisons come up far short of their intended purpose. You see, our Good Shepherd doesn't have to wait until evening time to take inventory to find out if one sheep is missing and then go out into the wilderness to find it. If one of His sheep is in the wilderness, He knows about it before it ever happens, and He doesn't have to go into the wilderness—if His sheep is there, He is there, "for he hath said, I will never leave thee, nor forsake thee" (Hebrews 13:5). He is the all-knowing (omniscient), ever-present (omnipresent), indwelling Christ.

In my human weakness and inability to adequately describe Him, I cease trying and say,

> Hallelujah! what a Saviour!
> Hallelujah! what a friend!
>
> Saving, helping, keeping, loving,
> He is with me to the end.[28]

---

28. J. Wilbur Chapman, "Our Great Saviour," Refrain.

The LORD is my shepherd

One writer of Scottish descent wrote,

> This psalm really has nothing to do with you if you don't know the Shepherd of whom the psalm speaks. One of the saddest things in my life as a minister is this. I have to attend many funerals and, very frequently, funerals of people who know nothing about the Shepherd. And inevitably in Scotland they want us to sing Psalm 23. There are godless people at funerals who will sing "The Lord's my Shepherd," and in the ugly presence of death and the solemn reality of eternity, they will take comfort from this that does not belong to them.[29]

Dr. J. Wilbur Chapman in his book *The Secret of a Happy Day* wrote,

> Martin Luther once said that most of experimental religion would be found in the personal and possessive pronouns of the Bible, and that is certainly true of this psalm, for here we find only six verses, and they contain only one hundred and eighteen words, and in this brief list twenty-eight pronouns may be counted. . . .
>
> [The] appropriation of Him in the use of this little personal pronoun "my". . . will bring rejoicing where otherwise there would be despair; it will inspire a song where there might have been a groan; it will put a silver lining on every cloud; it will gird you with strength for every temptation. . . . This little word will make a paradise of

29. MacMillan, *The Lord Our Shepherd*, 36-37.

earth, and fill with glory the home where you live and the place where you work; in a word, it will lift you up to the heavenlies.[30]

My shepherd—what a word it is!

Little words are sometimes very important. Suppose you read Psalm 23:1 thus: "The LORD is **a** shepherd." Would it mean the same to you? The name Shepherd may carry in itself all of its wonders of love, tenderness, care, and safety as a picture of God; but what comfort would that be if you could not say, "The LORD *is* **my** shepherd"?

Some poor children, passing a beautiful home with its wealth and luxury, may admire it and say, "What a beautiful home!" But how much more it means to the children who live there, who say, as they enjoy the good things in the house, "This is my home!"

It makes a great difference to me whether I can say a good man is a worthy friend or is my friend; whether God is a Father or is my Father; whether Jesus is a wonderful Saviour or is my Saviour; whether the Lord is a Shepherd or is my Shepherd.

Some years ago a certain church in a town in Derbyshire was holding its Sunday school anniversary when the local member of Parliament, a godless man was induced to attend. Something happened to him at that service that completely altered his whole life and future. Let me once more (for almost every preacher has told the story, or at least the first part of it—the Scotch part; though the Derbyshire part is almost unknown) recount

30. 21–22.

the familiar tale. The preacher that day said that a man taking his holiday in Scotland came upon a shepherd boy in a field minding the flock. Sitting down beside him the stranger presently asked him if he knew the Twenty-third Psalm. Of course he did: he was a Scotch boy! "Then, what is the opening sentence?" "The LORD is my shepherd." "Say it again now, ticking off a finger for each word." "The—LORD—is—my—shepherd." Then came some earnest words from the Christian man explaining how, by definitely accepting Him as our Saviour and Lord, we can have Him for our own. There and then in that field on that lovely quiet summer morning the lad did for himself "receive" Him (John 1:12); and before the two separated, the shepherd boy said the words over again, finger by finger, this time clutching hard at the fourth. "The—LORD—is—*MY*—Shepherd." The succeeding winter was a severe one; and it so happened that one day the snow had fallen very heavily, and neither the boy nor his sheep came home—they were all caught and buried in a deep drift. When they came to dig, they discovered the bodies of many dead sheep, and presently they came on the wee laddie—quite dead, lying on his back, peace on his face, the fourth finger of his left hand grasped by his right hand. Such was his last thought and such his hope for eternal years. That was the story the preacher told in the Derbyshire church that day, which deeply impressed the godless M.P.. And the sequel? That immediately, the man was quite changed in outlook and behavior giving evidence that something had happened inside; and some years later the man died in his bed, and when they turned down the sheet they found his right hand holding the fourth finger of his left.

Oh, the difference that "*MY*" makes! A little group of boys were discussing a pocket-knife that was being passed around among them. One boy said, "What a lovely knife"; another said, "What an expensive knife"; a third said, "What a useful knife"; a fourth, "What a sharp knife"; as each passed it longingly along. As it came back to the last boy in the circle, he said, "Yes, it's *my* knife!" So he was in the fortunate position of being able to enjoy all its values for himself. Oh yes, . . . He is "the good shepherd"; . . . He is "that great shepherd"; and He is "the chief shepherd"; all so wonderfully and gloriously true, but Psalm 23:1 says He is "*my* shepherd"—the One Who has suffered for me and sought me and saved me and satisfied me and sheltered me and so much else![31]

If the Lord would allow us to read between the lines, or get all the implications in the statement, "The LORD *is* my shepherd," I believe we would find an implied question that other sheep would have to answer. In my imagination I can hear David saying, "Who is your shepherd? The LORD is mine!" And because He is my Shepherd *I shall not want.*

---

31. King, *All Through the Day*, 17–19.

We draw from that truth an application to our contentment in Jesus Christ, our wonderful Lord, and say with confidence that the man-made religions of this world have nothing we want. *The Lord Is My Shepherd, and That's Enough!*

I shall not want

Others, far wealthier and wiser than I, may want, but *I shall not.* "The young lions do lack, and suffer hunger: but they that seek the Lord shall not want any good *thing.*" [Psalm 34:10]. It is not only "I do not want," but "*I shall not want.*" Come what may, if famine should devastate the land, or calamity destroy the city, "*I shall not want.*" Old age with its feebleness shall not bring me any lack, and even death with its gloom shall not find me destitute. I have all things and abound; not because I have a good store of money in the bank, not because I have skill and wit with which to win my bread, but because "*The LORD is my shepherd.*"[32]

Dr. H. O. Van Gilder once said something like this—

If the green pastures in which you have been feeding are suddenly scorched to the roots by the withering sun of adversity, or if the shade tree under which you have been sitting at the side of a wilderness oasis is split from top to bottom by a sudden shaft of lightning, and that which you had hoped to be your shelter for years to come is suddenly laid waste around you, you have a Shepherd

---

32. Spurgeon, *The Treasury of David, Part 1*, 354.

who knows where there are other green pastures and other still waters.[33]

I shall not want because He knows me.

We have many times heard the story of the census taker asking questions of the mother of a large family. "How many children do you have?"

The mother replied, "Well, there is Johnny, Bobby, Thomas, Susan, Martha . . ."

"Never mind the names! Just give me the number."

The mother replied, "My children don't have numbers, they all have names."

Jesus said in John 10:14, "I am the good shepherd, and know my sheep." And in John 10:3 we read, "He calleth his own sheep by name."

Some commentators like to use the words of Jesus to make the claim that in Bible times shepherds knew all of their sheep by name. Maybe a shepherd with only a few sheep could have named each one, but when we consider that Job had 7,000 sheep at the beginning of and another 14,000 at the end of his life's story, Moab gave the king of Israel 100,000 lambs, the Israelites avenged themselves of the Midianites and took 675,000 sheep, and Solomon sacrificed 120,000 sheep at the dedication of the Temple (see Job 1:3; 42:12, 2 Kings 3:4, Numbers 31:32, and 1 Kings 8:63), we cannot imagine each and every sheep having its own name and that each of these was remembered by its owner, but neither can we imagine an omniscient Shepherd

33. Van Gilder, paraphrased in Ketcham, *I Shall Not Want*, 14.

who cannot remember our names. The LORD Himself said to Israel, "I have called *thee* by thy name; thou *art* mine" (Isaiah 43:1).

In the early days of the twentieth century, Bible teacher William Evans said,

> A photograph was placed on my desk. It had inscribed on it a number, but no name. It was the likeness of a convict. It was a number I went to jail to see; a number I spoke with by the cell door; a number I stood by and saw handcuffed; a number with whom I walked down the steps of the jail; a number with whom I walked up the stairs to the scaffold; a number around whose neck I saw the rope placed; a number I saw drop to his death.
>
> Sin degrades personality, but the religion of Christ exalts its adherents to a place in that innumerable company which cannot be numbered, but every one of whom bears upon his forehead the name of his Redeemer and King. Jesus calleth His sheep by name, not by number.[34]

It is comforting to know that we have a Shepherd who knows our name, but that's not all—He knows our needs. The Scriptures declare,

> For the LORD thy God hath blessed thee in all the works of thy hand: **he knoweth thy walking through this great wilderness**: these forty years the LORD thy God *hath been* with thee; thou hast lacked nothing. (Deuteronomy 2:7)

---

34. *The Shepherd Psalm: A Meditation*, location 168–174.

Shall not God search this out? for **he knoweth the secrets of the heart**. (Psalm 44:21)

For **he knoweth our frame**; he remembereth that we *are* dust. (Psalm 103:14)

Many reports have been given about the familiarity and bond that was between the oriental shepherd and his sheep, and the most convenient way for the shepherd to remember his sheep was by their imperfections.

Evangelist Tilden Gaddis said this about the oriental shepherd—

He often distinguishes them by their blemishes. That one has a piece out of its ear; this one limps; another one toes in a little; one has lost a patch of wool, etc. I wonder if the Lord distinguishes some of His sheep that way.[35]

What was said about the Israelites while they were in Egyptian bondage can be said about His people in every age: "I have surely seen the affliction of my people which *are* in Egypt, and have heard their cry by reason of their taskmasters; for I know their sorrows" (Exodus 3:7).

In concluding our study of this first verse, if the reader can in all honesty say, "The LORD *is* my shepherd," acknowledging we are sheep and we belong to Him, then he can also say, "He that spared not his own Son, but delivered him up for us all, how shall he not with him also freely give us all things?" (Romans 8:32), and, "My God shall supply all your need according to his riches in glory by Christ Jesus" (Philippians 4:19).

So, our reader can further say with the psalmist, "I shall not want."

---

35. *The Shepherd Psalm*, 16.

Martha Walker Cook (1806–1874) wrote,

> In some way or other the Lord will provide.
> It may not be my way, it may not be thy way;
> And yet in His own way, "the Lord will provide."
>
> At some time or other the Lord will provide:
> It may not be my time, it may not be thy time;
> And yet in His own time, "the Lord will provide."
>
> Despond then no longer; the Lord will provide:
> And this be the token—no word He hath spoken
> Was ever yet broken: "The Lord will provide."
>
> March on then right boldly: the sea shall divide;
> The pathway made glorious, with shoutings victorious,
> We'll join in the chorus, "The Lord will provide."
>
> Then we'll trust in the Lord, and He will provide;
> Yes, we'll trust in the Lord, and He will provide.

Few people could tell of a life with more tragedy than Annie J. Flint who was born on Christmas Eve, in the year 1866 to the Johnson family. Just three years later, at the young age of 23, her mother passed away, and that began for Annie a life of heartache and heartbreak few people have ever experienced, but out of that life filled with tragedies came,

> He giveth more grace when the burdens grow greater,
> He sendeth more strength when the labors increase;

To added afflictions He addeth His mercy,
To multiplied trials, His multiplied peace.

When we have exhausted our store of endurance,
When our strength has failed ere the day is half-done,
When we reach the end of our hoarded resources
Our Father's full giving is only begun.

Fear not that thy need shall exceed His provision,
Our God ever yearns His resources to share;
Lean hard on the arm everlasting, availing;
The Father both thee and thy load will upbear.

His love has no limits, His grace has no measure,
His power no boundary known unto men;
For out of His infinite riches in Jesus
He giveth, and giveth, and giveth again.

He lays me where the green herbs grow

Along the quiet mead:

He leads me where the waters glide,

The waters soft and still,

Psalm 23:2

"He maketh me to lie down in green pastures: he leadeth me beside the still waters."

Once we get a picture in our minds of a lush, green pasture with a flock of those fluffy, white creatures—maybe some with a cute, little lamb grazing contentedly nearby—and the shepherd resting beneath the shade of a sprawling tree by a gently, flowing brook of clear, cool, refreshing water as he watches over those sheep, it's hard to see anything else, but if that is all we see, we miss a major lesson on the work of the shepherd.

John 10:4 explains it by stating, "When he putteth forth his own sheep, he goeth before them." A good shepherd did not turn his sheep into a grazing land unless he had already been there and made sure there was an ample supply of grass for the number of sheep that would be grazing. He checked the entire pasture for any poisonous grass or vegetation that would harm the sheep. If there were beasts of prey, they were run out and made to hide somewhere beyond the boundaries of the pasture land, and if he found vipers, they were killed, or a ring of oil was poured around their holes so they wouldn't crawl out and bite the sheep. There also had to be a sufficient supply of water—not just any water, but still waters—the only kind sheep would drink from.

William Knight shared the explanation given by his Syrian guest—

"He maketh me to lie down in green pastures," [which provides] nourishment [and] rest. [But when] "he leadeth me beside the still waters," the scene changes and so does the meaning. You think here of quietly flowing streams; so you get one more picture of rest; but you miss one of the finest scenes in shepherd life and one of the rarest blessings of the soul that is led of God. All through the day's roaming the shepherd keeps one thing in mind. He must lead his flock to a drinking-place. The refreshment of good water makes the coveted hour of all the day; the spot where it is found amid the rough, waterless hills and plains is the crowning token of the shepherd's unfailing thoughtfulness. When at last the sheep are led "beside the still waters," how good it is, after the dust and heat of the sheep-walks!

Would you get the shepherd meaning here? Then remember that streams are few in the shepherd country of Bible lands. The shepherds do not rely on them. Even where streams are found, their beds and banks are usually broken and their flow rough. Sheep are timid and fear a current of water, as they well may for they are easily carried down stream because of their wool.

. . . The sheep would indeed have a hard time finding water to drink, were it not that the shepherd sees to that.

. . . Brother, you and I have learned how much is in that question and answer. How would we get the refreshment we need in the rough world, if the Shepherd did not see to that? But He does, He does![1]

There surely must have been a lot of scouting by the shepherd in finding the ideal pasture furnished with just what his sheep needed to thrive on, and the scouting was done by him alone and unnoticed by the sheep.

He maketh me to lie down

There are those who teach that a shepherd must be able to force the sheep to lie down, even against their will, but that thought is the result of omitting the little word *to*, as many of the modern translations of the Scripture do.

One writer in error, declares that

Perhaps they [the sheep] . . . do not want to rest, so he *makes* them "to lie down in green pastures."

. . . Our slogan becomes "Activity," and so for our good He touches "the hollow of our thigh" and causes us to rest.[2]

When God made sheep He gave them a nature **to** rest in the place the shepherd has supplied. Almost every commentator, or shepherd writer, will remind us there are times when sheep won't lie down. Those times are when there is frustration in the flock, when they are afraid of some predator, when they are agitated by insects such as nose flies, or when they are hungry, but when those problems are eradicated, the contented sheep will lie down.

---

1. *The Song of Our Syrian Guest.*
2. Slemming, *He Leadeth Me*, 35–36.

They do not have to be forced to lie down; they lie down because that's what God gave them a nature to do. Sheep are also made **to** chew the cud and grow wool, but one would consider a shepherd ignorant of a sheep's nature if he tried to force the sheep to chew the cud or grow some wool.

When God created the world, He gave certain creatures a nature **to** do certain things that He didn't give others. For example, I used to hear Dr. Bob Jones Sr., that very refined, cultured preacher and educator, say something like this—When God made a man He gave him a voice to call a hog with, but He gave a woman a voice with which to sing a lullaby to a baby. He gave a man hands to bridle a mule with, but He gave a woman hands with which to change a baby's diaper.

God made a dog **to** bark, a fish **to** swim, a bird **to** fly, a cow **to** sleep lying down, but a horse **to** sleep standing up, etc. And God's creatures do not have to be forced to do what they have a nature for—sheep do not have to be forced to lie down. They only need to be in the flock of a good shepherd who has made sure they are not being agitated by insects, that all the other sheep in the flock are at peace, that the wolf has been sent on his way, that they have been fed all the green grass they want, and that they have drunk from the still waters—then, and only then, will they lie down of their own accord. Why? Because that is what God made them **to** do. That's what they have a nature to do.

Now, just as other creatures have a desire for certain things, so man in his fallen, sinful state has a nature that is concerned with satisfying his carnal desires, but when we as poor, helpless, and hopeless sinners are brought face to face with our sinful condition, and

116

turn to the Good Shepherd that gave His life for the sheep, He makes us new creatures, so that old things are "passed away; behold, all things are become new" (2 Corinthians 5:17), He makes us "partakers of the divine nature" (2 Peter 1:4), and He admonishes us to "seek those things which are above, where Christ sitteth on the right hand of God" (Colossians 3:1).

For to be carnally minded *is* death; but to be spiritually minded *is* life and peace. Because the carnal mind *is* enmity against God: for it is not subject to the law of God, neither indeed can be. So then they that are in the flesh cannot please God. But ye are not in the flesh, but in the Spirit, if so be that the Spirit of God dwell in you. Now if any man have not the Spirit of Christ, he is none of his. (Romans 8:6–9)

Some, when speaking of the many who profess to know Christ, wonder why their lives are no different than any other child of this world.

Here is a short story of a little, pet pig that illustrates perfectly why some never have a changed life—

A pig on a leash

There are, alas, some who pass among their fellows for saved sheep while, in reality, they are but washed swine. You must have heard the legend of the Chinese Emperor's little pet pig. He had, from its birth, brought it up to be so completely different from all others of its ilk [kind]. It was daily washed, and beautifully clothed, and faddishly fed—all piggish tastes and habits were eradicated from its nature. Often, on a lead, it would accompany its Imperial Master on his walks abroad, the little pet the delight of passers-by. One day, while thus linked together they happened to be at a place where, in the near distance, was an evil muddy puddle. All of a sudden there was a sniff and a snort, there was a violent tug at the unprepared leash and the perfect little gentleman was off! Before they could stop it, it was rolling in the mud: its pig's heart hadn't been changed. A stupid tale; but a solemn truth. Many I say again, appear to be sheep who are swine still; and when they slip back into evil ways people mistakenly refer to them as backsliders when, as a matter of fact, they never were Christians at all; spectators look criticizingly on and sneeringly observe that these "results" never last, when, in truth, they have never actually begun. As 2 Peter 2:22 says, "It is happened unto them according to the true proverb, The dog *is* turned to his own vomit again; and the sow that was washed to her wallowing in the mire." You see, my illustration is a scriptural one; and it behooves us all to make quite sure that we are indeed His sheep before we pass on to think over what it means to have His shepherding care.[3]

And Spurgeon added to the pig on a leash story these very powerful and truthful words—

---

3. King, *All through the Day,* 13.

No man has the right to consider himself the Lord's sheep unless his nature has been renewed, for the scriptural description of unconverted men does not picture them as sheep, but as wolves or goats.[4]

Green Pastures and Still Waters

The scene before us of the sheep lying down in the green pastures does not picture a one time, or even an occasional, abnormal, or unexpected experience, but rather a day by day, each and every day experience of satisfaction from the supply of the shepherd who was able to do exceeding abundantly above all that the sheep needed.

Since David's Shepherd is also my Shepherd, I too have the privilege of the same day by day experience of the green pastures described by Spurgeon in these words—

What are these "green pastures" but the Scriptures of truth—always fresh, always rich, and never exhausted? There is no fear of biting the bare ground where the grass is long enough for the flock to lie down in it. Sweet and full are the doctrines of the Gospel; fit food for souls, as tender grass is natural nutriment for sheep. When by faith we are enabled to find rest in the promises, we are like the sheep that lie down in the midst of the pasture; we find at the same moment both provender and peace, rest and refreshment, serenity and satisfaction.[5]

Dr. Ketcham declares that many people

4. *The Treasury of David (Part 1)*, 353.
5. Ibid., 354.

Have met the Saviour from sin's guilt in Psalm Twenty-two, but oh, how they need to meet Him as the Shepherd of Psalm Twenty-three!

The over-all picture of the great mass of professing Christians today is appalling. Instead of looking out upon a host of God's own dear ones "rest[ing] in the LORD and wait[ing] patiently for him" (Psalm 37:7), we see a crowd of poor, scared, nervous, tired, and weary sheep. There is no rest. . . . The slightest strange sound, and the sheep are "jittery." The constant bleating of restlessness is heard throughout the flock of God.

The blessed Shepherd is heard to be saying again and again, "Fear not, little flock" (Luke 12:32), but the sheep are afraid to trust Him.

Poor, tired, weary and hungry sheep! How they need to know that the presence of the Shepherd is a guarantee of safety! How they need to know that He is able and sufficient for *any* danger, and if they will but "lie down" and *rest* and eat in peace, He will "work for them that wait for Him"! This is the "peace of God" which keeps "hearts and minds" in a place of sweet rest from day to day.[6]

Still waters

We have already established the fact that God gives each creature its own unique nature and temperament, and one of the traits of

---

6. *I Shall Not Want*, 19.

sheep is that they will not drink from rapid-flowing or noisy, turbulent water.

MacMillan, the shepherd from Scotland, gives us this first-hand information—

> A sheep will never drink out of a fast-flowing stream.
> . . . When we were bringing our sheep into the farm,
> . . . coming from the farthest corner of our hill, we used
> to have to ford two streams or "wee burns" with them;
> . . . the sheep would sometimes be so thirsty that their
> tongues would literally be hanging out. However, at the
> first stream we forded there was a lot of gravel and stones.
> It was a fast-flowing stream, with many ripples, and not
> a single sheep—not even a thirsty one—would stop to
> drink in it, . . . but the next stream we came to, just half
> a mile further on, was a very broad ford where the water
> hardly moved, and at these "still" waters *every* sheep
> would stop and drink.[7]

The water was on the grass.

It is also well known by those familiar with sheep that they take in very little water, especially if they have grazed in the early morning hours of the day after the green pastures have been drenched with dew. The necessary water was on the grass, and the sheep got both at the same time. However, if the grass was dry, and there was no other water supply, the sheep could not survive.

---

7. *The Lord Our Shepherd*, 90.

MacMillan gives another incident of a sheep that had been missing for several days, and when they found her she was on a big ledge of rock about six or seven feet down from the top that had some green grass on it. She had jumped down and nibbled the grass away, but she couldn't jump back up. The shepherd said,

She had plenty to eat, but nothing to drink, and although we had managed to rescue her, she died two days later. Why? Well, I opened her up and found that all the grass she had eaten had hardened into a solid ball. Ultimately, instead of nourishing her, it had choked life out because there was no fluid. She was . . . completely dehydrated, and she could not use the food she had eaten.[8]

It is very obvious that pastures without water will not sustain the life of sheep; neither will the letter of the law provide strength for the inner man of a Christian without the Holy Spirit.

Mr. Thomas Dale makes this truth very clear—

With guidance to "green pastures," therefore, the psalmist has, with good reason, associated guardianship beside "still waters": for as we can *only* appropriate the word through the Spirit, so we shall principally receive the Spirit through the word. . . . The Spirit of God . . . will come into the heart of the believer, . . . [and] the effect of His coming will ever be, the realization of some promise, the recognition of some principle, the attainment of some grace, the understanding of some mystery, which is already in the word, and which we shall thus find, with

8. Ibid., 91.

a deeper impression, and with a fuller development, brought home with power to the heart.[9]

Ruminating

A sheep's stomach has four different parts. The rumen is the largest part and is referred to by some as a *fermentation vat* where the food the sheep has eaten earlier ferments.

A wise shepherd, if the pastures are available, will get his flock into the grazing grounds long before the break of day, and while the dew is still on the grass the sheep will eat until they want no more. Then when the sun rises and burns the dew off of the grass, they will lie down and regurgitate some of the contents of the rumen and, for several hours each day, repeatedly chew it. This is described as *ruminating*, but the Bible uses terminology a farm-boy can understand— *chewing the cud* (See Leviticus 11:1–8).

What the world calls meditation

One type of meditation is an offshoot of Hinduism practiced by sitting on a rubber mat with your legs and arms crossed trying to connect with yourself through controlled breathing and chanting a mantra. It is a pagan religious practice that has absolutely nothing to do with scriptural meditation.

One writer described meditation as mentally coughing up some facts or ideas previously taken in and sorting them into useful categories before applying them to real life situations.

---

9. *The Good Shepherd and the Chosen Flock*, 51–52.

Christians meditate.

Christians practice a mental type of "ruminating" when they *meditate*. The grazing grounds for any spirit-filled child of God is the pure and precious written Word of God. Hundreds of testimonials can be found in the biographies of obedient servants of Christ that show the best time to come before an open Bible with a prayer for the Holy Spirit to shed light on the Scriptures is in the early hours of the day. It has been said that "the rudder for the day is set in the first hour."

Psalms 110:3 says, "Thy people *shall be* willing in the day of thy power, in the beauties of holiness **from the womb of the morning: thou hast the dew of thy youth.**"

The "dew" is a type of the Holy Ghost and "thy youth" is a type of strength or power. When does the dew fall? It falls early in the morning.

We could find no better example of how to start our day than with our Good Shepherd—"And in the morning, rising up a great while before day, he [the Lord Jesus Christ] went out, and departed into a solitary place, and there prayed" (Mark 1:35).

Many times, as a preacher meditates on a certain passage of Scripture that he read earlier, a sermon will take shape or maybe some old truth will come to mind which will help him make some wise decisions. On the other hand many sermons that are filled with calculated information, logically arranged, and delivered with precise diction and inflections produce no fruit because they are powerless and are preached from a heart which has no warmth.

In my opinion the psalmist described the right kind of preaching when he said, "My heart was hot within me, **while I was musing** the fire burned: *then* spake I with my tongue" (Psalm 39:3).

I am afraid the note in a church bulletin describing the faulty heating system could also describe some Sunday sermons. It simply read, "The heat is off but the blower is still on."

Even the rule book for success—the Bible—declares,

This book of the law shall not depart out of thy mouth; but thou shalt **meditate** therein day and night, that thou mayest observe to do according to all that is written therein: for then thou shalt make thy way prosperous, and then thou shalt have good success. (Joshua 1:8)

And Psalm 1 declares,

Blessed *is* the man that walketh not in the counsel of the ungodly, nor standeth in the way of sinners, nor sitteth in the seat of the scornful. But his delight *is* in the law of the LORD; and in his law doth he **meditate** day and night. And he shall be like a tree planted by the rivers of water, that bringeth forth his fruit in his season; his leaf also shall not wither; and whatsoever he doeth shall prosper. (Psalm 1:1–3)

Of course, the inventions of men available today provide us with a continual flow of information—whether true or false. According to Thomas M. Nichols, "Ideas crowd in upon us in such profusion that we have no time to sort them."[10]

---

10. Nichols, *Preaching*, 27.

Contentment

A more peaceful scene could hardly be imagined—helpless sheep lying in an overabundance of what the shepherd has supplied who have no worry about their safety or provision for tomorrow.

Notice the simplicity.

In Psalm 23:2, it only took two items to satisfy the sheep—grass and water. The Apostle Paul said, "And having food and raiment let us be therewith content" (1 Timothy 6:8).

» When God led the children of Israel on their forty year journey through the wilderness, He supplied their daily bread—manna and quail (Psalm 78:25).

» When the prophet Elijah was at the brook Cherith, the Lord sent the ravens twice a day with bread and flesh (1 Kings 17:6).

» When Elijah obeyed the voice of the Lord and made a visit to the widow woman in Zarephath, she took her last bit of meal and her little portion of oil and made the prophet a meal. God then blessed her with a continual supply of meal and oil (1 Kings 17:15).

» Jesus once fed a multitude of more than five thousand with five loaves and two fishes (Luke 9:10–17).

» On another occasion Jesus fed four thousand with seven loaves and a few fishes (Mark 8:1–9).

» When the resurrected Christ revealed Himself to the Emmaus disciples and the eleven disciples gathered in Jerusalem, He asked them, "Have ye here any meat? And they gave him a piece of broiled fish, and of an honeycomb" (Luke 24:41–42).

» When some of the disciples had fished all night on the sea of Tiberias and caught nothing, Jesus provided them with the miracle of the fish-laden net. Then He invited them to, "Come *and* dine" and served them bread and fish from an early morning breakfast He had prepared for them (John 21:12–13).

» When the Apostle Paul was on his final journey to Rome, the people on the ship fasted for fourteen days because of their terror of the storms and the danger. Paul encouraged them to break their fast and eat something saying, "This is for your health." The people then ate bread and meat (Acts 27:33–36).

» When a church observes the "Lord's Supper," each individual who partakes with an honest heart, is saying, "By taking the *bread* and the *wine* (just two items), I am in communion with Christ who gave His *body* which was broken and His *blood* (just two items) which was shed as the redemptive price for mankind."

It is very obvious that Scripture does not encourage a complicated lifestyle, and the last reference to the Lord's Supper indicates Christ never meant for our fellowship with Him to be complicated.

Just two items, grass and water, was all it took to satisfy the sheep, but in this day of greed and self-centered living, people have more worldly possessions than ever before, but along with their possessions there is less contentment than in the history of the world.

Discontentment gives birth to greed, and our modern society is filled with it because one woman was convinced by Satan that she needed more than what God had provided. She fell for the lie, ate the forbidden fruit, and then gave it to Adam, and so the fall of man took place. Then 4,000 years later Paul wrote, "But I fear, lest by any means, as the serpent beguiled Eve through his subtilty, so your minds should be corrupted from the simplicity that is in Christ" (2 Corinthians 11:3).

Money

The love of money is declared to be "the root of all evil: which while some coveted after, they have erred from the faith, and pierced themselves through with many sorrows" (1 Timothy 6:10).

Hopefully, some of the great and powerful verses warning against the deceitfulness of riches will help some reader to forsake the American dream and get back to the simplicity which is in Christ.

King Solomon was the wisest and wealthiest man that ever lived, and in his old age he gave these words of wisdom—

He that loveth silver shall not be satisfied with silver; nor **he that loveth abundance** with increase: this *is* also vanity. . . . The sleep of a labouring man *is* sweet, whether he eat little or much: but **the abundance of the rich will not suffer him to sleep.** (Ecclesiastes 5:10, 12)

In Luke 12:15, we find the Good Shepherd Himself saying, "Take heed, and beware of covetousness: for **a man's life consisteth not in the abundance of the things which he possesseth.**"

Adam Clarke once said, "It requires but little of this world's goods to satisfy a man who feels himself to be a citizen of another country."[11]

---

11. Clarke, *Clarke on the Whole Bible,* location 199154.

Christ, and none but He, satisfies desires.

There is a restless, a boundless desire in the mind of man for something which this world in all its glory is unable to bestow. This immortal appetite, this living desire, blinded mortals seek to gratify—some with honor, others with pleasure, some with riches, others with empire and glory. And need we therefore be surprised that they are never satisfied? Though I could trace my pedigree through illustrious heroes, and renowned kings, back to the first foundation of kingdoms, this would not furnish my soul with all it would desire. Though I had the knowledge of all educated men summed up in myself, so that the wisest philosophers might come and learn at my feet, still my desire would have its void to fill. Though I had all magnificent titles, honorary epithets, aggrandizing distinctions, and appellations of renown, even these would not fill the extensive blank. Though I had the uncontrolled dominion of the whole universe devolved [transferred] on me, so that my name were revered in every nation, statues set up to me in all lands, and my fame and glory echoed through every kingdom, still would my desires be making new demands. Though Arabia, as my possession, should present me all her fragrant spices, the Indies, as my inheritance, amass for me all their riches, and all kingdoms, as tributary, send me their wares; though the earth should burst open all her silver veins and golden mines to enrich my treasures;

though my throne were of one pearl, and my crown of one diamond; though my guards were kings, my menial servants princes, and my immediate subjects nobles; though the daily guests of my table were thousands and ten thousands of honorable personages; and though, for the entertainment of my table, my flocks should cover every hill, my herds range over every flowery valley, and the fowls of every wing alight around my palace, while the fish of every fin came, when needed, spontaneously ashore; though the fountains should flow with oil, the rivers stream with wine, and the forests drop honey— yet my heart would not say, "It is enough!" . . .

Where, then, is this all-sufficient plenitude to be found? or what is it that will satiate my immense desires? A triune God reconciled to me in his own Son, and conveying Himself to me, in the infinite plenitude of his spiritual riches; and the eternal portion of my immortal soul.

All the gathered parts of creation—knowledge, titles, honor, riches, renown, attendants, dependants, family, friends, dominion, health, longevity, and every other excellence—are but like a drop to my parched soul, of which I could swallow many, and yet be altogether faint beneath the scorching beam. But Christ is an ocean of overflowing fullness! I stand on this shore, and am astonished! I look, and in its boundless extension lose myself! I possess, and am replenished—so that I can desire no more. . . . All things without Christ cannot give satisfaction; for truly without Christ all things are nothing—but, with him what seems next to nothing is more and better than the worldling's all things! Material things, however excellent, do not suit; and cannot satisfy the immaterial and immortal soul.

But in Christ there is something that satiates, refreshes, and enraptures the believing soul, even when my prospect is towards that tremendous day, when nature shall be set on flames; or further still, towards eternity, where the creature dares not present itself as a proper portion for the soul. "In him dwelleth all the fulness of the Godhead bodily" (Colossians 2:9). My desires are complete in him. I can go no further, I can wish no more than he has. Then, for the present, I am happier than the happiest worldling, having a heaven in possession! While a heaven of rapture and delight, floods of ecstasy and bliss, are in reserve for me![12]

There used to be an advertisement for a certain brand of cigarettes that said "they satisfy." The late Evangelist Lester Roloff said, "If they satisfy, why did they put twenty in a pack?" He would then go on to preach about how it should only take one Jesus, one salvation, one Bible, etc., to satisfy a Christian.

---

12. Meikle, *Solitude Sweetened*, 125–127.

And homeward He will gently guide
My wandering heart and will.
He brings me on the righteous path,
E'en for His Name's dear sake.

Psalm 23:3

"He restoreth my soul: he leadeth me in the paths of righteousness for his name's sake."

Restoreth, in its simplest form, means "to bring back to a former and useful state," yet from this one word with such a simple definition, we see more love, longsuffering, forgiveness, faithfulness, and ability of the shepherd than in any other action he could take toward the sheep, and from the experience David had in seeking wayward sheep and getting them back on the right path, he saw a parallel with the way our Lord treats us who are the sheep of His pasture.

At times the action a shepherd had to take in restoring a wayward sheep was very time-consuming and expensive, and in some cases one wandering or sick sheep restored to the fold or back to good health would never be able to produce enough wool to pay for the trouble it had caused; but there was more at stake than monetary gain. The shepherd's reputation of loving sheep was on the line, and a healthy, happy flock was his trademark. We who truly know the Lord Jesus Christ as our Good Shepherd, regardless of how many guidelines for life He lays down or how severe any chastisement He may have put us through in order to keep us on the path of righteousness, are a testimony, not to what good sheep we are, but to what a good shepherd He is.

Reasons for and Methods of Restoration

A crook for the lambs

Though there are no shepherds' "crooks" mentioned in Scripture, the history of sheep and shepherds, and manners and customs of Israel in Bible times tells us the shepherd's staff, curved into a hook on one end, became a crook. Then when the shepherd noticed a baby lamb wandering in the wrong direction or trapped in the briars or maybe fallen into some ravine, he would hook the end of his staff around the back leg of the lamb and gently pull it back to safety. He might even stop long enough to scratch the lamb's head, or maybe tickle it under the chin before restoring it to its mother.

At other times there would be a sheep just a short distance from the flock, but headed in the wrong direction. The shepherd would use his sling to drop a stone just a few inches in front of the sheep's nose, and the stone would startle it enough to turn it around and send it running back to the flock. But if the sheep, unaware of its own wandering, would get out of the view of the shepherd, the shepherd would secure the safety of all the other sheep and would go seek the one missing until he found it.

It might be an easy find with a simple solution. The wayward sheep could just be over the knoll, moving along aimlessly, and by giving one simple call the shepherd would be able to chase the sheep back to the fold. On the other hand, the shepherd might find it far away, already attacked by some beast of prey, seriously injured but still alive. This last was experienced by David when he once had to deliver a lamb out of the mouth of a bear and a lion (see 1 Samuel

17:34–36). The good shepherd would rescue the sheep, put it on his shoulder, and carry it back to the fold. It might take several weeks of special treatment from the shepherd for the injured sheep to completely recover, and it might carry some scars from its wayward experience for the rest of its life, but it would be restored to its former position with the flock.

Too much of a good thing

Another time the sheep may need restoration is when they wander aimlessly while nibbling a bit of grass at a time with no concern about which direction they are headed.

Robert Ketcham observed,

It is not always the sheep's nibbling in "wild" grass that gets it into trouble, but more frequently it is the persistent nibbling in "good" grass, which results in a conscious separation from the presence of the shepherd. It is true that many of God's children find themselves out of fellowship with the Shepherd by reason of worldliness, or "wild" grass in their lives. But it is our observation that far more of them are living in a place where they do not realize the blessed presence of the Shepherd because of their occupation with, and concentration upon, actually good things.

The pastor may become busy with sermon preparation and pastoral calling, and a thousand other things, all of them good in themselves. But if they become the dominant things in his life, he will find himself altogether too frequently "on the other side of the knoll," and will have to know the experience of the Shepherd coming to him, and either gently or otherwise, bringing him back into fellowship with Himself. Preoccupation with "things," even good things, may become disastrous. Fellowship with the Shepherd is victory.[1]

The cast sheep

One of the major problems and dangers with sheep is when they become cast (unable to get up on their own).

MacMillan said,

The sheep that wanted the easy bed was always in danger, because she would lie down and sometimes stretch her legs, and then the balance of equilibrium would be lost and she could not get her feet back on to the ground. She would scrape the ground and sometimes tear up all the grass, but she could not get back on to her feet. The longer she lay there the greater her danger. Gases would build up, causing tension, making the sheep blow out and cutting off the blood supply, especially to the place where she needed it most—her legs. . . .

You see this in Christians too—the Christian who is out for the easy option, who wants the soft number in life. The shepherd who becomes wise to the fact that the sheep looks for a soft hollow chases her out of it, and

---

1. *I Shall Not Want*, 27.

Christ will do the same. He will not allow you to have a soft option; he knows the danger this is for you.[2]

Too much wool

Another cause of sheep becoming cast is when they have too much wool. Sheep should be sheared at least once a year, and since the sheep and the wool both belong to the shepherd, the sheep doesn't resent its owner taking what belongs to him (see Isaiah 53:7). However, before shearing time there is a danger to a perfectly healthy sheep. If the wool gets wet and loaded with foreign matter, it can become so heavy that when the sheep lies down she can't regain her footing. Figuratively speaking, many Christians have a lot of wool, or material blessings (especially riches) that become their downfall. David's son, Solomon, who was recognized as the richest and wisest man alive in his day, said, "There is a sore evil *which* I have seen under the sun, *namely*, riches kept for the owners thereof to their hurt" (Ecclesiastes 5:13).

One shepherd told of finding a ewe that had been cast long enough for the blood circulation to her legs to almost stop. When he got her onto her feet she could hardly stand alone, so he straddled her and held her up so he could rub her legs to help the circulation. After helping her take a few short steps, she began to walk by herself. Then, with a wagging tail, she frolicked and bounced like a playful baby lamb and ran back to the flock with a "Baaa, baaa," as if to say in sheep language,

---

2. *The Lord Our Shepherd*, 94–95.

I've wandered far away from God . . .

My soul is sick, my heart is sore,
Now I'm coming home;
My strength renew, my hope restore:
Lord, I'm coming home.[3]

The discontented troublemaker

The inquisitive, discontented sheep seems to be one of the most difficult to ever break from the bad habit of habitually straying into forbidden territory. Keller told of one of his prize ewes which had that one bad habit. She looked until she found a loophole, and even at the expense of grazing in far less desirable grass, she had to wander away from the rest of the flock. Time after time he brought her back to the fold only to find her missing just as soon as she found a way to escape. When some of the other sheep started following her example, and her own baby lambs began to follow her, he knew it was time for her to go, so with a big, killing knife he butchered her.

Any good shepherd will rejoice over a healthy, contented flock of sheep, but he will also love a wayward and disobedient sheep and go to whatever measures necessary to correct any problem that sheep may have. However, when the sheep itself becomes a problem for the other sheep, their very lives are in danger.

Some writers tell us at the entrance of some of the larger sheepfolds sat a pot of dye. When the shepherd stepped aside to allow the sheep to file through the door one by one, he would watch for the

3. Kirkpatrick, "Lord, I'm Coming Home," stanza 1a & 4

troublemaker he had given up on to walk by. When it did he would dip the end of his rod in the dye and rake a streak down its side—it had been marked for the kill.

The very familiar analogy used by most commentators to show the difference in being led by a good shepherd or being driven by a stranger was given to me personally by a friend who hosted tours to the Holy Land. One day in Israel he noticed a flock of sheep with orange marks on their backs being driven instead of being led. He inquired as to why the man was driving his sheep instead of leading them, and the gentleman replied, "I am not a shepherd. I am a butcher, and these sheep are being taken to the slaughterhouse." The orange mark on each sheep's back was evidence it had, for one reason or another, been identified as a non-productive sheep and marked for the kill.

Now friend, you can rest assured if an earthly shepherd will not allow even one sheep to ignore his leading, our Good Shepherd who gave His very life for us will not look the other way while we do our own thing.

Since there is such a shallow brand of Christianity in our day, it seems a little difficult to find a parallel between the way a shepherd would not let those in his flock get away with going in the wrong direction compared to many of those who profess to know Christ as their Saviour, and yet live their lives with little or no regard for church, the Bible, prayer, or anything holy at all—yet there is never any indication of correction in their lives. They have adopted the old antinomian doctrine that says the Gospel in the heart is all that matters. Standards, rules, or regulations to govern one's life are of no importance to them. Some groups call it the "grace principle" which is just an excuse for saying, "I am a sheep, but I refuse to be brought under the complete care and control of the Good Shepherd."

If the reader happens to fall into this category, consider these very, stern words from Scripture—

> My son, despise not thou the chastening of the Lord, nor faint when thou art rebuked of him: For whom the Lord loveth he chasteneth, and scourgeth every son whom he receiveth. If ye endure chastening, God dealeth with you as with sons; for what son is he whom the father chasteneth not? But **if ye be without chastisement, whereof all are partakers, then are ye bastards, and not sons.** (Hebrews 12:5–8)

Marked for the kill

I once talked with an inmate on death row in an Alabama prison. His bunk had an open Bible lying on it. On the walls of his cell were some pictures of his family, but mostly the walls were covered with handwritten verses of Scripture. Looking through the bars of the little cell he called "home" that was smaller than a public parking space, with a very humble attitude and tenderness in his voice, he told me in his own words how as a young man in a church service in Montgomery, Alabama, he had truly trusted Christ as his Lord and Saviour, but in later years he became rebellious and wandered so far from God that his sin brought him all the way to death row—he too had been marked for the kill.

At times Satan will tell a Christian just one little look toward the world; just one little fling in the night; just one bite of the forbidden fruit will be no big deal. But regardless of how innocent the devil's lie may sound, if we ignore the instructions and warnings the Holy Spirit places in our path, though it will not always be met with death, the consequences (at the discretion of the Good Shepherd) will always be severe enough to bring about the restoration intended by our Good Shepherd. The results will remind us for the rest of our lives that disobedience will not be tolerated.

Don't ignore the warning.

I recently heard a preacher tell the story of a lady whose neighbor had a solid, block fence between their properties. Hanging on the fence was a sign that said, "WARNING: BAD DOG! KEEP OUT!" Curiosity got the best of her so she ignored the warning and stood on a small stool and peered over the fence. A vicious pit bull on the neighbor's side of the fence was able to lunge high enough to sink his sharp teeth into her face, breaking bones and ripping away flesh that left her with scars for life. I never researched for the validity of the story, but true or false, the principle is the same. If you are one of the Lord's sheep, you cannot ignore the warnings He places in your path and not suffer the consequences—but even with the consequences, there comes the peaceable fruit of righteousness.

Prone to wander

Another word of caution to some who might think of themselves more highly than they ought to think. You can never gain a position in the flock that guarantees you will never stray from the right path.

For example, back in the 1700s Robert Robinson of London, England, was greatly influenced by the great evangelist, George Whitefield. Robinson was converted, studied for the ministry and became a very successful pastor. However,

> in the latter part of his life, [he] often indulged in frivolous habits. But on one occasion, while traveling in a stagecoach, he encountered a lady who soon compelled him to admit his acquaintance with religion. She had just been reading this hymn ["Come Thou Fount of Every Blessing"], and she asked his opinion of it, after having told him of the blessings it had brought to her heart. He avoided the subject and turned her attention to some other topic; but the lady, who did not know to whom she was talking, soon returned to the hymn, expressing her strong admiration for its sentiments. Agitated beyond the power of controlling his emotion, Robinson broke out: "Madam, I am the poor, unhappy man who composed that hymn many years ago, and I would give a thousand worlds, if I had them, to enjoy the feelings I had then."[4]

---

4. Sankey, *My Life Story*, 74.

Come Thou Fount of Every Blessing

Jesus sought me when a stranger,
Wandering from the fold of God;
He, to rescue me from danger,
Interposed His precious blood;

How His kindness yet pursues me
Mortal tongue can never tell,
Clothed in flesh, till death shall loose me
I cannot proclaim it well.

O to grace how great a debtor
Daily I'm constrained to be!
Let Thy goodness, like a fetter,
Bind my wandering heart to Thee.

Prone to wander, Lord, I feel it,
Prone to leave the God I love;
Here's my heart, O take and seal it,
Seal it for Thy courts above.

Though we don't have much information about how the composer of this great old hymn ended his journey through this world, there are reports of him preaching sermons that declared the deity of Christ and the glory of God, a strong indication that he was restored to the ministry of preaching Christ.

The sick sheep

For our final thoughts on the restoration of the sheep, we turn our attention to the one in the flock who has never strayed, and in the view of all the others is perfectly normal, but to the shepherd with a skillful eye, that one sheep is just not as healthy as the rest of the flock. That sheep may have eaten some noxious grass or been infested with parasites or contracted some disease peculiar to sheep that is keeping it from producing good quality wool. Its steps are slower than usual, and it is no longer alert and attentive to the shepherd. Long before these symptoms showed up, the shepherd knew this sheep had a problem because it began to lose its appetite, and shepherds tell us that is the first sign of a sick sheep.

The restoration of the *sick sheep* gives us a better analogy of the restoration of a *sick saint* than all of the other ways and reasons for restoring the sheep, because this is the only one that has to do with an inward problem. Just like the wise and able shepherd knows how to treat his ailing sheep, so our Good Shepherd knows how to treat His sheep that are not doing so well.

Where Does the Work of Restoration Take Place?

He restoreth my soul.

The soul is the inner man where the mind, emotions, desires, passions, conscience, memory, and life itself resides. In Scripture the soul and the heart are synonymous terms. Therefore David could express "he restoreth my **soul**" by these words—"My **heart** is fixed, O God, my **heart** is fixed" (Psalm 57:7; 108:1).

144

One very able preacher of our day has a classic sermon he preaches titled, "*The Heart of the Problem, is the Problem of the Heart.*"

We can find no authentic record of who said it first, but we do agree with the old cliché, "If it ain't broke, don't fix it!" The attitude of many in this Laodicean age is, "I am rich, and increased with goods, and have need of nothing." But God says, ". . . and knowest not that thou art wretched, and miserable, and poor, and blind, and naked" (Revelation 3:17).

Through the years I have known many who seemed to be in perfect health, but one visit to an emergency room with sudden and unexpected chest pains and shortness of breath revealed that a major heart attack was in progress, and within a short time they were called into eternity. They didn't know they had a very serious heart condition, and so it is with unsaved people who see no need for the services of the great Physician.

Jeremiah 17:9 declares that, "The heart *is* deceitful above all *things*, and desperately wicked: who can know it?" But as long as depraved humanity continues to believe their heart is okay, God will not intervene. He will not fix that which is not broken!

Also, like there are sheep that have a lot of internal problems which are not detected by the other sheep, so a truly born-again Christian may have the idols of this world as the centerpiece of their lives; yet other Christians, especially ones in the same spiritual condition, may see these believers as pillars of the assembly. If they could see the inner man, what a contrast there would be between their profession and their possession.

145

There is a fruitful, victorious, Spirit-filled Christian life that comes through total consecration to the will of God, but as long as one lives for self, he will not be filled with the fruit of the Spirit, and he will never experience a day by day walk with Christ.

Any man, saved or lost, who hears the Word but allows the cares of this world and the deceitfulness of riches to choke out that Word in his heart, will surely become unfruitful.

The best of preachers will lay heavy emphasis on the importance of starting each new day with a time of prayer and Bible reading, but if the reader feels that his short time of personal devotions in the early morning hours will keep him spiritual while he spends the rest of the day trying to satisfy addictions to social networking, texting, Hollywood entertainment, professional sports figures, materialism, etc., he is only deceiving himself.

If there happens to be a reader who has picked up some poison—maybe through the influence of some worldly acquaintance, possibly in the form of false doctrine, maybe through just one click of a computer mouse—you have wandered into forbidden territory. Maybe you have been convinced the American dream is the end of the rainbow, and if you can just get enough of this world's goods, that will erase all of the problems you will ever encounter, and life will be one big celebration of what you have achieved. This is a big misconception, and as previously stated, the Scriptures declare, "Because thou sayest, I am rich, and increased with goods, and have need of nothing; and knowest not that thou art wretched, and miserable, and poor, and blind, and naked" (Revelation 3:17).

Reader, maybe you once knew a life of victory in Christ, but somehow old man "self"—the carnal, Adamic nature—has mounted the throne of your life, and all the happiness he promised is not there. Is there any hope for restoration? YES! There is hope, but only if the old man is reckoned dead, and he must die every day (see 1 Corinthians 15:31).

The Apostle Paul described the life of a spiritually healthy Christian in these words—

> I am crucified with Christ: nevertheless I live; yet not
> I, but Christ liveth in me: and the life which I now live in
> the flesh I live by the faith of the Son of God, who loved
> me, and gave himself for me. (Galatians 2:20)

If one seeks to be like Christ, the starting place would be to pray like He did, "Not my will, but thine, be done" (Luke 22:42).

> I asked the Lord for some motto sweet,
> Some rule of life with which to guide my feet.
> I asked, and paused. He answered soft and low,
> "God's will to know."
>
> "Will knowledge then suffice, dear Lord?" I cried.
> But ere the question into silence died—
> "Nay, this remember, too.
> God's will to do."
>
> Once more I asked, "Is there no more to tell?"
> And once again the answer sweetly fell,

"Yes, this one thing—all other things above—
God's will to love."[5]

Restoration Illustrated

With Naomi

The book of Ruth is the story of a famine in Bethlehemjudah that drove Elimelech to take his wife Naomi, and two sons, Mahlon and Chilion, to the land of Moab. After the sons had married Moabitish girls, Elimelech and his two sons died, leaving his wife Naomi in a strange land with nothing but a broken heart and two Moabitish daughters-in-law, Orpah and Ruth.

Somehow Naomi heard there was bread back in her homeland so she made preparation to return to Bethlehemjudah. She informed Orpah and Ruth of her plans and encouraged them both to return to their gods and stay in Moab, but Ruth would have none of it. She said,

> Intreat me not to leave thee, *or* to return from following
> after thee: for whither thou goest, I will go; and where
> thou lodgest, I will lodge: thy people *shall be* my people,
> and thy God my God: Where thou diest, will I die, and
> there will I be buried: the LORD do so to me, and more
> also, *if ought* but death part thee and me. When she saw
> that she was stedfastly minded to go with her, then she
> left speaking unto her. So they two went until they came
> to Bethlehem. And it came to pass, when they were come

_____

5. *I Shall Not Want*, 32.

148

to Bethlehem, that all the city was moved about them, and they said, *Is* this Naomi? And she said unto them, Call me not Naomi, call me Mara: for the Almighty hath dealt very bitterly with me. I went out full, and the LORD hath brought me home again empty: why *then* call ye me Naomi, seeing the LORD hath testified against me, and the Almighty hath afflicted me? (Ruth 1:16–21)

Naomi was getting up in years. She was too old to have a husband and past the age of bearing children: the only thing she had was a daughter-in-law who she would rather have had stay in Moab. Ruth was so poor she had to get on God's welfare program.

God had told the Israelites,

And when ye reap the harvest of your land, thou shalt not wholly reap the corners of thy field, neither shalt thou gather the gleanings of thy harvest. And thou shalt not glean thy vineyard, neither shalt thou gather *every* grape of thy vineyard; **thou shalt leave them for the poor and stranger**: I *am* the LORD your God. (Leviticus 19:9–10)

After only one day of gleaning in the field, Ruth came home with more than enough barley for both herself and her mother-in-law, and when Naomi saw all that barley, she said,

Where hast thou gleaned to day? and where wroughtest thou? blessed be he that did take knowledge of thee. And she shewed her mother in law with whom she had wrought, and said, The man's name with whom I wrought to day *is* Boaz. (Ruth 2:19)

149

At this point we see a little ray of hope in the words of Naomi, and for us who know the rest of the story, we see the beginning of the ministry of restoration.

It was only a few days until a courtship between Boaz and Ruth was in full swing. Then

> Boaz took Ruth, and she was his wife: and when he went in unto her, the LORD gave her conception, and she bare a son. And the women said unto Naomi, Blessed *be* the LORD, which hath not left thee this day without a kinsman, that his name may be famous in Israel. And he shall be unto thee a **restorer** of *thy* life, and a nourisher of thine old age: for thy daughter in law, which loveth thee, which is better to thee than seven sons, hath born him. And Naomi took the child, and laid it in her bosom, and became nurse unto it. And the women her neighbours gave it a name, saying, There is a son born to Naomi; and they called his name Obed: he *is* the father of Jesse, the father of David. (Ruth 4:13–17)

When David penned the words "he restoreth my soul," he was without doubt referring to the analogy found in the way he treated his sheep, knowing God takes the same care of His sheep. But he also had an illustration in his ancestry. Naomi, David's great-grandmother, had gone from a poor, broken-hearted widow in Moab to the family of a mighty man of wealth, and finally to the lineage of the King. That's restoration!

With Job

We need not speculate on the character of Job because God Himself said, "*There is* none like him in the earth, a perfect and an upright man, one that feareth God, and escheweth evil" (Job 2:3), but regardless of how much integrity Job had maintained, in short order he lost 11,500 animals, ten children and all of his servants. He also lost the support of his wife. And while Job was smitten with sore boils from the sole of his feet to the crown of his head, and sitting in an ash pile scraping himself with a potsherd, his "friends" came to mourn with him, but his flesh was so distorted from the boils and the scraping of the potsherd, he was unrecognizable. His appearance was so gross they were speechless.

If there ever was a time Job needed to hear from the Lord, it was at this point in his life. However, in Job 3:1–2 we read, "After this opened Job his mouth, . . . and Job spake," and for the next twenty-eight chapters there is a dialogue between him and his three friends, with Job doing most of the talking. But one thing he was not able to do—he could not get God into the conversation.

In addition to all the burdens that had come into Job's life, he thought God had also become his enemy and wouldn't even speak to him. Where does one turn to after he has exhausted all of his reasoning and has found no explanation for the hardships that have come his way and when God seems to be uninterested in his dilemma? In Job's situation there was nowhere to turn, so he came to the end of himself, and we read the last six words in Job 31, "The words of Job are ended."

Job had nothing else to say, and once he came to that place, God sent His man, Elihu, to preach a six chapter sermon revealing to Job his real condition. During all of the accusations Elihu made toward him, Job never one time rebelled or talked back to God's messenger. He accepted everything Elihu said, and then we read in Job 38:1, "The LORD answered Job." God proceeded to ask Job some very pointed questions, and just as Elihu had given Job an opportunity to defend himself, God gave Job an invitation to speak for himself—

> Moreover the LORD answered Job, and said, Shall he that contendeth with the Almighty instruct *him*? he that reproveth God, let him answer it. Then Job answered the LORD, and said, Behold, **I am vile**; what shall I answer thee? I will lay mine hand upon my mouth. (Job 40:1–4)

As God takes Job further and further into the experience of understanding more and more about how great He really is, Job's conclusion is, "I have heard of thee by the hearing of the ear: but now mine eye seeth thee. Wherefore **I abhor** *myself*, and repent in dust and ashes" (Job 42:5–6).

Commenting on this great truth, Dr. Martin Lloyd Jones once said, "He who thinks well of himself, has never met God."

Job had experienced bereavement, financial losses, rejection by his friends, and a loss of physical health, but his biggest problem was a battle with self. Now we see him here—a broken and empty vessel.

At this point we can get some more light on how God implements His ministry of restoration from Jeremiah. We read,

> I went down to the potter's house, and, behold, he wrought a work on the wheels. And the vessel that he

152

made of clay was marred in the hand of the potter: so he made it again another vessel, as seemed good to the potter to make *it*. (Jeremiah 18:3–4)

Only a casual reading of the last few verses of the book of Job is needed to show how God took him, a broken man who had come to the end of himself, and restored him, not only to his former condition, but to a better and more prosperous life than ever before: "So the LORD blessed the latter end of Job more than his beginning: for he had fourteen thousand sheep, and six thousand camels, and a thousand yoke of oxen, and a thousand she asses" (Job 42:12).

The number of animals listed was exactly twice what was recorded at the beginning of Job's story, and we might safely assume since verse 10 says, "The LORD gave Job **twice as much** as he had before," that He was not only referring to the amount of animals, but also twice the amount of land to care for the animals, plus all the family blessings back in place and good health to enjoy them.

Our English definition of restoration doesn't quite measure up to all that God does when "He restoreth my soul." God demonstrated His definition of restoration to Job when He gave Job "exceeding abundantly above all that we [he could] ask or think" (see Ephesians 3:20).

The Apostle Peter

While examining the fact that God's definition of restoration is so much greater than our minds can comprehend, let us now consider the ministry of Peter.

Jesus asked His disciples,

Whom do men say that I the Son of man am? And they said, Some *say that thou art* John the Baptist: some, Elias; and others, Jeremias, or one of the prophets. He saith unto them, But whom say ye that I am? And Simon Peter answered and said, Thou art the Christ, the Son of the living God. (Matthew 16:13–16)

Peter had earned his reputation for being outspoken and impulsive, but in this instance when all of the other disciples only said what they had heard, he did the right thing and publicly confessed the truth about Christ. However, a little later on Peter's carnal nature revealed itself. When Jesus got closer to the hour of His trial and crucifixion, He said,

All ye shall be offended because of me this night: ... [but] Peter answered and said unto him, Though all *men* shall be offended because of thee, *yet* will I never be offended. Jesus said unto him, Verily I say unto thee, That this night, before the cock crow, thou shalt deny me thrice. Peter said unto him, Though I should die with thee, yet will I not deny thee. Likewise also said all the disciples. (Matthew 26:31–35)

Immediately after uttering these words and telling Peter what he would do in the near future, Jesus went to Gethsemane to pray while His disciples slept. He was then arrested and taken to Caiaphas, the High priest, and Peter followed, but he followed "afar off." Caiaphas then accused Jesus of blasphemy, and those present began to spit in His face, to buffet Him, and to strike Him with the palms of their hands. While this was going on,

154

Peter sat without in the palace: and a damsel came unto him, saying, Thou also wast with Jesus of Galilee. But he denied before *them* all, saying, I know not what thou sayest. And when he was gone out into the porch, another *maid* saw him, and said unto them that were there, This *fellow* was also with Jesus of Nazareth. And again he denied with an oath, I do not know the man. And after a while came unto *him* they that stood by, and said to Peter, Surely thou also art *one* of them; for thy speech bewrayeth thee. Then began he to curse and to swear, *saying*, I know not the man. And immediately the cock crew. And Peter remembered the word of Jesus, which said unto him, Before the cock crow, thou shalt deny me thrice. **And he went out, and wept bitterly**. (Matthew 26:69–75)

Luke included a very touching circumstance omitted by the other writers: "And the Lord turned, and **looked upon Peter. And Peter remembered the word of the Lord**" (Luke 22:61).

They were in the same room—Jesus at the upper end of the hall, elevated for a tribunal, and Peter below with the servants; so that Jesus could look down upon Peter standing near the fire. By a tender and compassionate look—a single glance of his eye—the injured Saviour brought to remembrance all Peter's promises, his own predictions, and the great guilt of the disciple; he overwhelmed him with the remembrance of his sin, and pierced his heart through with many sorrows. The consciousness of deep and awful guilt rushed over Peter's soul; he flew from the palace, he went alone in the darkness of the night, and *wept bitterly.*

The fall of Peter is one of the most melancholy instances of depravity ever committed in our world. But a little while before, so confident; seated at the table of the Lord; distinguished, throughout the ministry of Christ, with peculiar favours; cautioned against this very thing; yet so soon denying him, forgetting his promises; and profanely calling on God to witness what he knew to be false, that he did not know him! Had it been but *once*, it would have been awful guilt—guilt deeply piercing the Redeemer's soul in the day of trial; but it was three times repeated, and at last with profane cursing and swearing.[6]

One can only imagine the agony Peter suffered knowing he had just denied the One whom he had earlier confessed to be the Christ— the Son of the living God. Peter, no doubt thought that his discipleship was over, but sometime between this failure and the day of Pentecost (less than two months time) he was converted, or *restored*, not only to a former state, but to a far greater ministry than he could have ever dreamed. He preached one sermon, saw three thousand people saved, and later on wrote two divinely inspired epistles that bare his name and are included in the Bible.

Many times there are object lessons in the Scriptures we will not understand until we put ourselves in the shoes of the writer. For example, when Peter, a converted, commercial fisherman, wrote, "But the God of all grace, who hath called us unto his eternal glory

6. Barnes, *Barnes' New Testament Notes*, location 14088.

by Christ Jesus, after that ye have suffered a while, **make you perfect**, stablish, strengthen, settle you" (1 Peter 5:10), he was using language that a fisherman would understand.

As Peter penned the words, "suffered a while," he was surely reliving that awful night when he said, "I know not the man," but he very quickly added, "**make you perfect**."

This phrase has the same meaning as "to mend," when a fisherman *restores* a marred net back to a useful condition. So, to paraphrase Peter's words "make you perfect," we would say, "God is able to mend your net."

Peter understood that a marred net (or a net with a hole in it) would not catch fish so that net would be put on the shelf. But if the fisherman who owned the net ever took it off of the shelf and tied the broken strings back together, replacing some with newer and stronger ones, the finished *restoration* would make the net better than new. The fisherman would never mend a net if he didn't plan to use it to catch more fish.

Peter's initial call to the ministry is recorded in Matthew 4—

> And Jesus, walking by the sea of Galilee, saw two brethren, Simon called Peter, and Andrew his brother, casting a net into the sea: for they were fishers. And he saith unto them, Follow me, and I will make you fishers of men. And they straightway left *their* nets, and followed him. (Matthew 4:18–20)

At that point Peter became a net in the hands of the Master— "And going on from thence, he saw other two brethren, James *the son* of Zebedee, and John his brother, in a ship with Zebedee their father, **mending their nets**" (v. 21).

The very first day of following Christ, Jesus showed Peter a marred net that was being mended, and though Peter didn't see all that was illustrated for his future life, once he had the experience of failing his Lord but then being *restored* to fellowship and a ministry that brought multitudes of people to Christ, he was able to write that the God of all grace would "make you perfect," or "mend your net."

We have only chosen three people, Naomi, Job, and Peter as scriptural illustrations of the ministry of restoration, but many more could be given—such as Israel restored to her homeland; the clay in the potter's hand restored to a useful vessel; Jonah restored to a preaching ministry; Gomer restored to the family of Hosea; John Mark restored to the ministry, and on and on we could go. Then there could be volumes written from church history of saints who failed the Lord so miserably their hope of ever being used in any kind of service for Christ was at a low ebb, but God in grace and mercy gave each of them a second chance and turned the tide of their life and *restored* them to a life that pleased Him.

He leadeth me in the paths of righteousness for his name's sake

The goal of restoration

Every restored member of the flock of Christ . . . is restored not only to peace, but to purity—not only to happiness, but to holiness—not only to safety, but to

158

obedience! . . . [The psalmist] could not only affirm, as an instance of his Shepherd's kindness, "He restoreth my soul," but he could also add, as proof of the reality of his own restoration, "He leadeth me in the paths of righteousness for his name's sake."

These comprehensive words direct our attention to three fundamental doctrines of the sacred Scriptures. . . . First, . . . they point out the nature of that great blessing which the Lord confers upon His people: "He leadeth me." Secondly, they show us where He invariably leads them: "in the paths of righteousness." And lastly, they reveal to us the reason why the Lord thus leads His people in the paths of righteousness, "for his name's sake."[7]

He leadeth me.

MacMillan the shepherd said,

A sheep does not make straight tracks for itself. If you see sheep walking in a straight line, you can be sure of one thing: the shepherd is driving them or leading them. The wonderful thing about walking in obedience to God is this, that we are being led.[8]

Many times, especially from younger converts, questions about how to live the Christian life often surface with words like, "How can I be sure of which way is the right way?" or "How can I know if I am on the right path?"

7. Stevenson, *The Lord Our Shepherd*, 105–106.
8. MacMillan, *The Lord Our Shepherd*, 97.

The Bible is saturated with instructions for the Christian life, but for now we will only refer to one passage that should settle the issue forever—

> Wherewithal shall a young man cleanse his way? by taking heed *thereto* according to thy word. With my whole heart have I sought thee: O let me not wander from thy commandments. Thy word have I hid in mine heart, that I might not sin against thee. (Psalm 119:9–11)

Psalm 119:105 declares, "Thy word *is* a lamp unto my feet, and a light unto my path."

Those who try to navigate through this world without the guidance of the Scriptures are like travelers with roadmaps which have no route numbers or names of cities—just a lot of colored lines indicating roads with no reference as to their direction or destination. Among such careless travelers will be those who believe in the phrase, "let your conscience be your guide." The prophet Jeremiah rightly said, "O LORD, I know that the way of man *is* not in himself: *it is* not in man that walketh to direct his steps" (Jeremiah 10:23).

In this present evil world, there are two very distinctly different roads that men are traveling. One is the broad way "that **leadeth to destruction**," marked My own way, and the other is the narrow way which "**leadeth unto life**," marked His own way (Matthew 7:13–14).

People who insist on going their own way rather than trusting the Bible are like the man who lost his life savings in a business scheme that had been elaborately explained by a swindler. When his finances disappeared, he went to the Better Business Bureau.

"Why on earth didn't you come to us first?" the official asked. "Didn't you know about the Better Business Bureau?"

"Oh, yes," said the man sadly. "I've always known about you. I didn't come because I was afraid you'd tell me not to do it."

The folly of human nature is that even though we know where the answers lie—God's Word—we don't turn there for fear of what it will say.

Where are you headed?

One of the great differences between the two paths all men are traveling is their destination. The path of righteousness leads to "rest for your souls" or to green pastures and still waters, while the broad way is filled with immoral, dishonest, hateful, and deceitful men whose end is destruction.

> For many walk, of whom I have told you often, and now tell you even weeping, *that they are* the enemies of the cross of Christ: **Whose end *is* destruction**, whose God *is their* belly, and *whose* glory *is* in their shame, who mind earthly things. (Philippians 3:18–19)

The contrast between the two classes of people and their final destinations is very vivid in these good verses—

> And I saw a new heaven and a new earth: for the first heaven and the first earth were passed away; and there was no more sea. And I John saw the holy city, new Jerusalem, coming down from God out of heaven, prepared as a bride adorned for her husband. And I heard a great voice out of heaven saying, Behold, the tabernacle

161

of God *is* with men, and he will dwell with them, and they shall be his people, and God himself shall be with them, *and be* their God. And God shall wipe away all tears from their eyes; and there shall be no more death, neither sorrow, nor crying, neither shall there be any more pain: for the former things are passed away. And he that sat upon the throne said, Behold, I make all things new. And he said unto me, Write: for these words are true and faithful. And he said unto me, It is done. I am Alpha and Omega, the beginning and the end. I will give unto him that is athirst of the fountain of the water of life freely. He that overcometh shall inherit all things; and I will be his God, and he shall be my son. But the fearful, and unbelieving, and the abominable, and murderers, and whoremongers, and sorcerers, and idolaters, and all liars, shall have their part in the lake which burneth with fire and brimstone: which is the second death. (Revelation 21:1–8)

For our good and God's glory

There are so many blessings the Good Shepherd bestows on His sheep, and all of them are *for our good and His glory*.

The blessing for the sheep is seen in the words "**He leadeth me in the paths of righteousness.**" His glory is seen in the words "**for his name's sake.**"

Our Good Shepherd owns the sheep; therefore, "ye are not your own? For **ye are bought with a price**: therefore glorify God in your body, and in your spirit, which are God's" (1 Corinthians 6:19–20).

Just as a farmer's crop is a reflection of the ability and dedication of the farmer, so the quality of home-grown, fresh vegetables is a reflection of the knowledge and skill of the gardener. Also, a house is a reflection on the builder, a healthy patient is a good reference for a physician, and any other product is a testimony of the producer. Thus, the health, security, and safety of the sheep is a reflection on the shepherd.

In concluding this chapter let me suggest that the path of righteousness will not be that difficult to find, and walking therein can become your daily delight, but doing it all "for his name's sake" will take some dying to self.

I did!

Consider the following classic illustration of how we humans at least want a little bit of recognition for what we do—

A fable is told of two swans conversing with a bullfrog. "Have you ever seen the hidden beauties of my pond?" asked the frog.

"No," replied the swans. "We have never had anyone to guide us."

"Follow me," said the frog, as he plunged into the water and conducted the two birds on their sightseeing tour. When the swans surfaced for air, they asked the frog if he would like to see something of the beauties of the countryside. "But I cannot fly," said the frog. Then he added, "If you hold a stick in your beaks while I hang on with my mouth, you could carry me through the air and show me a world I have never seen."

The two birds agreed to this, and the journey started. They flew over hill and dale, revealing something of the glory of God's wonderful handiwork. As they came down low over a village, two shoppers happened to look up and see this astonishing sight. "Isn't that clever!" remarked one of them.

"Yes," replied the other, "I wonder who thought of that?"

The frog exclaimed, "*I did!*" and instantly dropped to the ground.

What if in vale and shade of death
My dreary way I take?
I fear no ill, for Thou, O God,
With me for ever art;
Thy shepherd's staff, Thy guiding rod,
'Tis they console my heart.

Psalm 23:4

"Yea, though I walk through the valley of the shadow of death, I will fear no evil: for thou art with me; thy rod and thy staff they comfort me."

F. B. Meyer on the Valley

In introducing our study of this fourth verse in this psalm, we would be hard-pressed to improve on F. B. Meyer's overall description of his view of "the valley of the shadow of death"—

Methinks I see that valley now. The Shepherd is conducting his flock towards their fold in luxuriant pastures, and in quiet resting-places. But suddenly the path turns downward, and begins to wind towards the ravine below. On the one side is a precipice, yawning in sheer descent to the steep riverbed, where the water foams and roars, torn by jagged rocks. On the other side the mountain firs cast a somber shadow in the deepening twilight. The path still plunges downward until it passes into a deep and narrow gorge, overhung by the frowning battlements of rock, which almost touch overhead; while the trees join hands, bough enclasping bough. It would be dark there in the most brilliant noon. To linger there after sundown would be to court the ague. All along its course are the lairs and haunts of ravenous beasts. Such is the valley of

167

the shadow of death, through which the Great Shepherd once went alone, and by which He now conducts all His flock to their Home. The foremost ranks have long ago emerged into the sunshine; others are now passing through its dark shadows; and ere long we, too, may be beneath them.

This figure gives us some comforting thoughts about death. It is not a state, an enduring condition, or an abiding place. It is a passage, a transition, a valley through which we walk. The valley may be darksome and lonely, and infested with evil things; but we do not pitch our tent there; we pass through it to our rest. In death the spirit leaves the body and passes out, just as an artisan will leave the workshop at the evening hour, shutting blinds and doors as he passes out to his home, and leaves it deserted and still; but his voice is to be heard in his home-circle, as he makes glad the wistful hearts that had waited for him; and whose joy had been incomplete till he came.[1]

It Is Going Down

Several sources give the description of an actual "Valley of the Shadow of Death" as a valley leading from Jerusalem to the Dead Sea. In places it is very narrow with side walls as high as 1,500 feet. It is less than five miles long, but in that short distance it drops from 2,700 feet above sea level to 400 feet below sea level.

---

1. *Shepherd Psalm*, 34–35.

This valley was a very convenient path for getting the sheep to the green pastures and still waters, but it was also the most dangerous one. Because the very rocky, jagged side walls were extremely narrow and very deep, it got very limited direct sunlight which provided an abundance of shadows where robbers could hide while waiting for an opportunity to attack a shepherd, or where beasts of prey could hide unnoticed and pounce on their victim.

Grazing conditions in Palestine would change with the seasons, and according to Adrian Rogers,

> shepherds would lead their sheep through [this] valley
> to Jericho where the grass was green even in the winter-
> time. When spring would come, the shepherds would
> lead their sheep through the valley to green pastures in
> the highlands.

Rogers went on to say, "No doubt David led his sheep through this 'valley of the shadow of death.'"[2]

Reason tells us that helpless, dependent sheep would have had no chance at all of making it all the way through that dangerous, treacherous valley without the aid of a wise and able shepherd. David was that kind of shepherd, but he knew there was a much bigger valley, called "this life" that winds its way through this present evil world, and like the disciples who once were caught in the midst of a troubled sea, and cried out, "Lord, save us: we perish" (Matthew 8:25), so each and every individual on Planet Earth must come to know the Good Shepherd who giveth His life for the sheep, or they too will perish in this valley of the shadow of death.

2. Rogers, *The Lord Is My Shepherd*, 64.

Four Analogies

Psalm 23 is called by some, the "psalm of the valley" because of its location between Psalm 22, which is a preview of Calvary where Jesus died and Psalm 24, a preview of the second coming of Christ to Mount Zion. Thus it runs all the way from the Cross to the Crown.

The next analogy is that all of the dark and dismal times in life—regardless of how insignificant or severe they may be—are represented by the valley of the shadow of death.

The third metaphor often referred to is that when the dreaded season of suffering and struggling with death itself finally arrives, one has entered the valley of the shadow of death.

While the three preceding comparisons should not be discredited—they all have their place and many good illustrations can be gleaned from those positions—the analogy that gives us the most scriptural applications is that the valley of the shadow of death is a description of the entire life span of each individual. Every person has their own life to live, and when a baby is first born into this world, he has entered his own "valley of the shadow of death." Even though the newborn begins to grow and mature physically, just like the valley of the shadow of death in Palestine follows a downward path that ends at the Dead Sea, so that baby, the moment he is born, starts his own journey through his own valley that will ultimately end in death. Though none of us can know for sure when that day of death will come, we can definitely be sure it will come.

When a newborn baby is only thirty days old, we can tear a one month page from his calendar of life. Each day, each month, and each year we all grow closer to the end of our days in the valley, and for those who can honestly claim the abiding presence of Christ, our Good Shepherd, we have nothing to fear—not even death itself.

We quoted earlier what Spurgeon had to say about David's attitude when he penned this psalm—

> Sitting under a spreading tree, with his flock around him, like Bunyan's shepherd boy in the Valley of Humiliation, we picture David singing this unrivalled pastoral with a heart as full of gladness as it could hold.[3]

If the valley of the shadow of death only represented the difficult seasons of life, then David would not have penned "Thou *art* with me" because he was not having a bad day. However, the good days didn't eliminate the bad days. I have many times heard this life referred to as "an *uneven* journey of life," and so it is. Good days and bad days come to us all, but the trusting sheep can live in constant peace that passeth all understanding and joy unspeakable because

> My Lord knows the way through the wilderness,
> All I have to do is follow![4]

In 1864, William B. Bradbury published that great old song, "He Leadeth Me," that perfectly expresses the attitude of a trusting child of God as he journeys through life—taking one day at a time, not knowing what tomorrow holds, but knowing who holds tomorrow.

> He leadeth me, O blessed thought!
> O words with heav'nly comfort fraught!

---

3. See p. 28.
4. Sidney Cox, "My Lord Knows the Way."

Whate'er I do, where'er I be
Still 'tis God's hand that leadeth me.

Sometimes 'mid scenes of deepest gloom,
Sometimes where Eden's bowers bloom,
By waters still, o'er troubled sea,
Still 'tis His hand that leadeth me.

Lord, I would place my hand in Thine,
Nor ever murmur nor repine;
Content, whatever lot I see,
Since 'tis my God that leadeth me.

And when my task on earth is done,
When by Thy grace the vict'ry's won,
E'en death's cold wave I will not flee,
Since God through Jordan leadeth me.

He leadeth me, He leadeth me,
By His own hand He leadeth me;
His faithful foll'wer I would be,
For by His hand He leadeth me.

Peace in the Valley

There may be those who only want God as a backup just in case trouble comes, but for the believer who is totally consecrated to the service of Christ, his joy is in consciously knowing the inward dwelling and constant abiding presence of Christ our Lord. The realization of the promise that "I am with you alway, *even* unto the end of the world. Amen" (Matthew 28:20) will produce within itself victorious Christian living.

Back in 1908, Anne Murphy said it well when she wrote,

> There's a peace in my heart that the world never gave,
> A peace it cannot take away;
> Though the trials of life may surround like a cloud,
> I've a peace that has come here to stay!

> *Constantly* abiding, Jesus is mine;
> *Constantly* abiding, rapture divine;
> He never leaves me lonely, whispers, oh, so kind:
> "I will never leave thee"—Jesus is mine.

Another great song that not only has great lyrics, but comes from the heart of one who knew something of the valley she sang about, is "In the Valley He Restoreth My Soul." According to the Dottie Rambo website,

> Dottie was born in 1934 in Madisonville, Kentucky, during the height of the Great Depression. She grew up in poverty. . . .
>
> At twelve years old, she became a born-again Christian and made a commitment to write and sing Christian music. The decision . . . did not sit well with her father who gave her an ultimatum—give up Christian music or leave. She left home and went on the road.[5]

---

5. Barry Drudge, "Biography," *Dottie Rambo*, accessed January 9, 2018, https://www.dottierambo.net/about/.

Without knowing all of the details from the rest of her story, we all know that for a young, teenage girl to be rejected by her own father for her commitment to Christ is a big valley to go through, but Dottie wrote and sang gospel music. According to her biography the Rambo family was one of the first gospel groups to sing in Vietnam for the American troops in 1967. But they didn't stop at the stage. Their hearts led them to the medical tents where men were hurt and dying. Dottie's family sang, prayed, and ministered to those who were hurt beyond repair. Nobody asked them to, but they went above and beyond the call of duty.

Dottie wrote and sang,

In the Valley He Restoreth My Soul

When I'm low in spirit I cry Lord lift me up
I want to go higher with Thee
But the Lord knows I can't live on a mountain
so He picked out a valley for me

It's dark as a dungeon
and the sun seldom shines
And I question Lord why must this be
Then He tells me there's strength in my sorrow
and there's victory in trials for me

And He leads me beside still waters
somewhere in the valley below
And He draws me aside

174

to be tested and tried

but in the valley He restoreth my soul.

Good Illustrations

My dad is the pilot.

The story has been told many times about the young boy enjoying an airplane ride, even during an intense storm. Each time there was strong turbulence, the plane would lose altitude and shake and buck as though it would come apart at any moment. It was plain to see that the passengers were becoming very uncomfortable, and even the flight attendants were showing signs of concern, but the young lad was perfectly calm and enjoying the ride. A passenger asked the boy if he was not afraid the plane would crash, to which he replied, "No sir, I'm not afraid because my daddy is the flight captain, and he knows how to get an airplane through a storm."

Keep your eyes on the Shepherd.

Author Allan Emery told of his evening visit with a shepherd in these words—

One night in a rugged area where the snows were recently melted and the grass was just turning green, I spent an evening with a shepherd and his flock. There were two-thousand sheep held on this lush mountainside for the night. The bonfire provided the means of preparing a good supper. Three dogs enjoyed bones near us. The sun had long since set and the vermilion sky had changed to burnt umber.

The sheep had quieted down, and then I heard it—the long wail of a coyote behind our camp. Across the arroyo [a dry creek] was an answering call. The dogs looked pleadingly at the shepherd for his consent to find the coyotes. The shepherd knew this is what the coyotes would like as the sheep would then be deprived of their protection. The sheep were on their feet now, and there was some bleating as the ewes brought their lambs close. The shepherd tossed some large logs on the fire, and the flames rose. In this light I looked out and saw thousands of little lights. I realized that these were reflections of the fire in the eyes of the sheep. In the midst of danger the sheep were not looking out into the darkness but were keeping their eyes set in the direction of their safety, looking toward the shepherd.[6]

The death of a loved one

In the New Testament the Apostle Paul described death as sleep and only a means of passing from mortality to immortality and from corruption to incorruption.

Behold, I shew you a mystery; We shall not all **sleep**, but we shall all be changed, In a moment, in the twinkling of an eye, at the last trump: for the trumpet shall sound, and the dead shall be raised incorruptible, and

6. *A Turtle on a Fencepost*, 53.

we shall be changed. For this corruptible must put on incorruption, and this mortal *must* put on immortality. So when this corruptible shall have put on incorruption, and this mortal shall have put on immortality, then shall be brought to pass the saying that is written, Death is swallowed up in victory. O death, where *is* thy sting? O grave, where *is* thy victory? (1 Corinthians 15:51–55)

The final test of a man's theology is how it measures up to death.

Thousands of testimonies of dying saints have been recorded, but from the many I choose the testimony of Allan C. Emery, Sr., whose own son said, "To us five children, [Daddy] represented strength, security, wisdom, loving concern, responsibility, authority, justice, and a living example of Christian life and witness."

In December of 1952, with the family gathered at his bedside, Mr. Emery drew his last breath, and Allan Jr., turned to his mother and said, "He's gone." Mother smiled and said, "What excitement at the eastern gate there must be."

Emery goes on to say,

That night the family doctor, who was raised as an orthodox Jew, said to me before leaving, "To me the final test of a man's theology is how it measures up to death. If you will give me a New Testament, I'll read it carefully."

Mr. Emery left these words and included them in his will as a witness for Christ—

I commit my soul into the hands of my Saviour in full confidence that, having redeemed it and washed it in His Most Precious Blood, He will present it faultless before the presence of my Heavenly Father, and I entreat my children to maintain and defend at all hazards and at any cost of personal sacrifice the blessed doctrine of complete atonement for sin through the Blood of Jesus Christ once offered and through that alone.[7]

He spit on her grave.

When our dear friends, Pastor and Mrs. Don Mangus, were told by the doctors that their little five-year-old girl had terminal leukemia they no doubt were heartbroken, as all of us would be. After the doctors had done all they could do, there came that dreaded realization they were living in the very shadow of death, and within a few days she was gone.

One day, a good, missionary friend, John Allen, and I visited what some would call the little "city of the dead" on the south side of Louisville, Kentucky. Brother Allen took me to the gravesite of his son, Ben, whom they had lost through a drowning accident at Pensacola Beach. He then told me of little Joy Elaine Mangus, and how that, when her father visited her grave, he would literally spit on that little mound of dirt and say, "You won't hold her long" and then would quote from the previous verse: "Death is swallowed up in victory. O death, where *is* thy sting? O grave, where *is* thy victory?"

---

7. *A Turtle on a Fencepost*, 86.

Life itself is a *big valley*, but within that *big valley* there are some *little valleys* that seem gigantic while we are going through them, but when they have run their course, we always find He was with us each and every step of the way and that they were for our good and God's glory.

In the following words the psalmist even recognized that the difficult days in our lives bring about good results: "Before I was afflicted I went astray: but now have I kept thy word" and "It is good for me that I have been afflicted; that I might learn thy statutes" (Psalm 119:67, 71).

In words that fishermen would understand, we say, "To realize the worth of the anchor, we need to feel the storm."

Lessons learned through blindness

To those familiar with the late Dr. Robert Ketcham, you know his eyesite was very poor, but in spite of the shadows in that valley, he maintained a very fruitful ministry and lived a victorious Christian life. Dr. Ketcham wrote this very enlightening experience about one of the more difficult times in his life—

> Since the second year of my ministry in 1913, it has been necessary for me to get print within a half-inch of my eyes before I am able to read it. The first nineteen years of my ministry it was necessary for me to memorize all my Scripture, all my hymns, all my pulpit announcements. . . . Upon the advice of my doctors a few years ago, I went to New York City where the world-renowned surgeon, Dr. Ramon Castroviejo, performed his famous

corneal transplant on my right eye. This is an operation where the cornea of the patient's eye is removed, and the cornea from the eye of some dead person is transplanted to the living eye. It is one of the most delicate operations known, and the percentage of success is not great. The discipline through which the patient must pass is terrible. For eight days and nights he must lie flat upon his back with his head clamped between sandbags so that he cannot move it so much as the fraction of an inch. He is not allowed to yawn, to sneeze, to cough, or make any other violent or semi-violent muscular movement. He is fed nothing but liquids, and very little of them. He lies with both eyes bandaged tightly shut for those eight days and nights. He is kept under powerful opiates and watched ceaselessly by nurses day and night to see that he does not make any sudden move which might ruin the delicate operation.

It was while I was lying flat on my back, in a world of darkness that could be felt, that the dear Lord so often spoke to my troubled heart and brought blessing out of what would otherwise have been complete and total ruin. What would the future hold for me? Would I be able to see again? Or would the operation be a total failure and would I lose what little sight I already possessed? Where were the thousands of dollars to come from to take care of these terrific hospital and doctor bills? If something went wrong with the operated eye, would it react upon the good eye through what is called sympathetic irritation and ruin the one that was not operated upon? Ten thousand questions like these went through my mind with express-train speed. Then I would cry out to the Lord and He would so wonderfully and sweetly still the raging waters.

One night as I was undergoing one of these times of testing, as I looked to the Lord for relief and victory, He seemed to speak to me *out of the darkness*, and impressions were left upon my mind that were so precious that I awakened my wife . . . and asked her to write [them] down before they escaped me. Here they are just as I dictated them to my wife at the three o'clock hour in the New York City hospital.

"These days we need to know the secret of being occupied only with Him and not with 'things.' Martha got into trouble worrying about 'things.' Mary got into blessing by being occupied with Him. As a *faithful* Shepherd our Lord *must* lead us into the *shadows* as well as in the *sunshine*. It is how we react that makes the difference between defeat and victory. If we become *preoccupied* with the *shadows*, we will become cynical, bitter, discouraged, and defeated. If we become *preoccupied* with the *sunshine*, we will be become self-satisfied, self-centered, thoughtless of others, and worse still, forgetful of *Him*. But if we remain *preoccupied* with the *Shepherd*, regardless of shadow *or* sunshine, we will survive *the peril of both* with Victory!"[8]

Man's greatest fear

Consider the article by John Lineberry in the June 30, 2017, issue of *The Sword of the Lord*—

A nationally prominent psychologist in his book on man's fear lists a total of 288 fears. . . . Some fear high places; others fear low places; while others fear being squeezed in too close a space. Here are some other fears: mysophobia (fear of dirt), hydrophobia (fear of water), nyctophobia (fear of darkness), taphophobia (fear of being buried alive), xenophobia (fear of strangers), hemotophobia (fear of blood), necrophobia (fear of the dead), triskaidekaphobia (fear of the number thirteen), algophobia (fear of pain), photophobia (fear of light).

Of all fears cited, six rise to the top: poverty, criticism, illness, old age, rejection, and death. He states that the fear of *rejection* is the greatest of all—stronger than death.

The most powerful influence on the younger generation is that of their peers. Why is it when an older sibling or a "friend" changes almost anything in their lifestyle, the younger ones, especially those in rebellion to their parents, will follow their example? It's because of the desire for *acceptance* or the fear of being *rejected*! But David wasn't influenced to write Psalm 23 out of peer pressure. I know that because of the singularity of each and every verse. A careful reading

8. *I Shall Not Want*, 22–24.

will show there is only one sheep and one Shepherd in Psalm 23, and that one sheep could say, "I will fear no evil [rejection included]: for thou *art* with me."

Stephen was rocked to sleep.

A classic example of being rejected for righteousness' sake is the account of wicked men stoning Stephen for his preaching—

> Ye stiffnecked and uncircumcised in heart and ears, ye
> do always resist the Holy Ghost: as your fathers *did*, so
> *do* ye. Which of the prophets have not your fathers per-
> secuted? and they have slain them which shewed before
> of the coming of the Just One; of whom ye have been now
> the betrayers and murderers: Who have received the law
> by the disposition of angels, and have not kept *it*. (Acts
> 7:51–53)

The result of such preaching was,

> When they heard these things, they were cut to the heart,
> and they gnashed on him with *their* teeth. . . . Then they
> cried out with a loud voice, and stopped their ears, and
> ran upon him with one accord, And cast *him* out of the
> city, and stoned *him*. (Acts 7:54–58)

Simply put, Stephen joined that great innumerable host of saints that have been rejected by wicked men.

> But he, being full of the Holy Ghost, looked up sted-
> fastly into heaven, and saw the glory of God, and Jesus
> standing on the right hand of God, And said, Behold, I
> see the heavens opened, and the Son of man standing

183

on the right hand of God. . . . And he kneeled down, and cried with a loud voice, Lord, lay not this sin to their charge. And when he had said this, he fell asleep. (Acts 7:55–56, 60)

I used to hear a dear preacher friend who loved to preach from the account of Stephen's homegoing say, "The enemies thought they stoned him to death, but in reality they only rocked him to sleep."

G. Campbell Morgan—REJECTED

G. Campbell Morgan was a highly respected and influential British evangelist. Before this, in 1888, he and one hundred forty-nine other young men sought entrance to the Wesleyan ministry. Though he passed the doctrinal examinations, he was then faced with the trial sermon. In a huge auditorium that could seat more than one thousand people sat three ministers and seventy-five others who came to listen. His heart sank as they regarded him with a critical eye. Two weeks after this sermon, Morgan's name appeared among the one hundred five rejected for the ministry that year.

Jill Morgan, his daughter-in-law, wrote in her book, *A Man of the Word,*

> He wired to his father the one word, "**Rejected**," and sat down to write in his diary: "Very dark everything seems. Still, He knoweth best." Quickly came the reply: "Rejected on earth. Accepted in Heaven. Dad."[9]

---

9. *A Man of the Word*, 60.

He promised never to leave me alone.

To illustrate the comfort that the ever-abiding presence of our Lord provides, Denis Lyle tells of this touching incident in the life of Ms. Helen Kuhn—

Helen Kuhn was the youngest of five children and had never known what it was to be alone. Her family always did things together. But there came a day when she found herself alone. Her parents died first and then her brother. Two of her sisters died exactly one month apart and the last of her three sisters had just died.

One of the things she dreaded was going back to an empty house. Previously, she didn't even have a key to the house. There had always been someone there to let her in. She was returning home and no one would be there. She drove the car into the garage and sat there for awhile, working up the courage to walk into the empty house *alone*. As she walked up the path, she prayed: "*O God, help me.*" As soon as she walked into the house, she turned the radio on just so there would be sound in those empty rooms. As she hung up her coat she caught the words that the *Old-Fashioned Revival Hour Quartet* was singing,

No, never alone, no, never alone,
He promised never to leave me,
Never to leave me alone.[10]

---

10. *From Earth to Glory*, 70.

The shadows in the valley

We must agree that the shadows in the valley do represent the more dangerous and disappointing times in life, but almost every commentary on Psalm 23 reminds us that the shadow of an enemy cannot hurt the sheep—the shadow of a dog, coyote, wolf, bear, lion, poisonous viper, or any other beast of prey cannot attack the sheep and bring physical harm. However, some who came through the shadow in their valley with no physical harm, came out of it with mental anguish, nervous breakdowns, and even chronic depression for the rest of their lives. In every illustration of one going through some dark shadow in life, there was some suffering. In all of my research, I only found one author declaring that *a shadow can hurt you*.

> Commentators are fond of telling us that the "shadows cannot hurt." That is but a shallow optimism playing with a poor platitude. It contradicts the facts of experience. Ask that worse than widowed wife, sitting in the shadow of her husband's crime, what she knows about it! Ask the children walking in the shadow of their parents' shame! Ask the husband standing in the shadow cast by the death of her who was the centre of all his interests and the source of all his comfort! Ask the multitude of the incapacitated, broken ere their prime—students, singers, artists, preachers—ask them if the shadow hurts! Nay, we do not need to ask. *The shadow does hurt.* Sometimes it kills.[11]

11. Freeman, *Life on the Uplands*, 82.

At this point the reader might think we are including information that should have been in the previous chapter, but before we could look at the following illustrations, we needed to get some understanding of the what causes some of the heartaches that cause so much suffering.

Any seasoned saint reading these lines could probably bring to memory some incident when a brother or sister in Christ got caught in the crossfire of a bitter battle between two inconsiderate "brethren" or maybe had to watch a full-blown church split or even through his own weakness he was overtaken in a fault.

Is there any hope for those that have been *hurt by the shadow?* Yes, there is hope!

> Brethren, if a man be overtaken in a fault, ye which are spiritual, **restore** such an one in the spirit of meekness; considering thyself, lest thou also be tempted. Bear ye one another's burdens, and so fulfil the law of Christ. (Galatians 6:1–2)

No, they won't come.

I am reminded of a dear, pastor friend who made a visit to the hospital where a little, naive teenage girl had just given birth to a baby out of wedlock. When the pastor walked into the room, she began to cry, and said "Oh, preacher, I didn't think you would come!"

His wise reply was, "Well, the baby is going to need a good church to attend." And with those simple, compassionate words, she knew her preacher was not condoning her sin, but giving her an opportunity for *restoration.* The preacher then asked, "Has your mom and dad been up to see the baby?" Her reply was, "No. They won't come!" How sad! There are a lot of people in this world who have been hurt by a shadow, and a little kindness will go a long way.

There is an old adage that says, "People don't care how much you know, until they know how much you care." One of the reasons so many professing saints never reach out to someone going through the valley is because they are in a dead, lifeless, and powerless church, and it is true, if you live in a cemetery long enough, you will stop crying when someone dies.

Shoeshine boy

Dr. James Crumpton used to tell the story of the sharply dressed businessman who took his seat in the barber chair. He then looked over at the little, colored shoeshine boy and said with an arrogant, demanding voice, "Shine 'em up n——— boy." Some people sure know how to be cruel! The little fellow began to cry, and the businessman said, "Well, I didn't mean to make you cry."

The boy replied, "You ain't done made me cry. These tears was already in my eyes. You jus' spoke sharply and made them come out. Since my mamma died, I ain't never been able to put flowers on her grave. If I'se can make enough money today, I'm gonna put flowers on Mamma's grave."

The business man said, "Well, I didn't understand." No, he didn't understand, and neither do we always know what someone is going through in secret. If we knew, we wouldn't be so quick to judge and condemn.

Telephone operator

Even though at this point of our study we are writing about *restoration*, the same compassion shown toward a suffering saint should be shown toward those who have never known Christ. This leads me to include another story told by Dr. Crumpton. Though this is not verbatim, I will tell it as well as I can remember—

There was a pastor who slept upstairs with his bedroom door closed and the heat off in the rest of the house. One morning, about 2 o'clock, the phone at the bottom of the stairs rang. The pastor pulled himself out of that warm bed and made his way down those chilly stairs. In those days there were telephone operators, and when the pastor answered the phone the operator said, "Sir, I am so sorry. I have dialed the wrong number."

The pastor replied, "That's all right, little lady. I understand." With that he made his way back up the stairs and into that warm bed.

Not more than fifteen minutes later the phone rang again, so the pastor pulled himself out of his warm bed and once again made his way down the chilly stairs to answer the phone. He heard the same operator say, "Sir, I am so sorry. I have called the wrong number again."

The pastor again replied, "That's all right, little lady. I understand," and he hung up the phone and went back upstairs to his warm, comfortable bed.

Not more than fifteen minutes later the phone rang again, and for the third time the pastor went down those chilly stairs to answer the phone only to hear the same operator say, "Sir I am so sorry. I have called the wrong number for the third time in a row—this has never happened to me before."

At this, the pastor again replied, "That's all right little lady, I understand"

And the operator then asked, "Are you a preacher?"

He replied, "Yes I am. How did you know?"

She said, "If I had called most people three times in a row, especially at this hour of the morning, they would have cursed me out, but when you were so kind, I thought 'He must be a preacher.'"

The preacher told her, "Little lady, I sure wish the worst mistake I ever made was dialing the wrong phone number three times in a row!"

Two weeks later that telephone operator came forward in that pastor's church, trusted Christ, and was saved. She then stood at the front of the church and told the congregation about her telephone experience with the pastor. She said, "That very morning I knew that if Jesus could make someone that compassionate and understanding, I needed to know Him."

Not only was the operator blessed by the attitude of the preacher, but the preacher was blessed with the opportunity to help someone in need.

Sad because he found no one he could help

A traveler, talking one evening with one of the monks of the St. Bernard Hospice of Switzerland, observed one of the famous dogs as, head down and tail drooping, it slunk by them to the kennels. "Is that dog ill?" he asked.

190

"No; it has happened to him on the mountain-side that he found no one to help, and he has come home so ashamed." No one to help—that could not be said of us; but, perhaps, this, that we did not help those we could. No wonder we are ashamed at sunset.[12]

We must see the great need of helping those who suffer from the shadows. For the dedicated saint of God, victorious Christian living is not being skillful in avoiding the shadows in the valley but in facing them. Victory can only come through staying close to the Shepherd, all the way to the end, and accepting the bad times as well as the good times.

My two feet

The story was once told of a soldier who, out of love for his country, volunteered his life through military service to defend her at any cost. On the battlefield he had both feet blown off at the same time.

When a friend came to his bedside and said, "I'm sorry about your injury," the soldier replied, "Don't feel bad. I gave my *life* to my country, but she only took my two feet."

I didn't lose it, I gave it.

A similar story is told about a soldier who had one arm blown off in battle. He was told by a friend, "I am sorry about the loss of your arm," and this soldier said, "I didn't lose it. I gave it."

---

12. King, *All Through the Day*, 71.

Thy rod and thy staff they comfort me

The rod

In ancient Israel when it was decided that a young lad was going to be a shepherd boy, he would dig from the ground a type of hardwood sapling that he would cut to the very length to fit his liking. It would be big enough to have very little flexibility, with a bulb-like knot at the bottom from which all the little feeder roots extended. He would remove all of these small roots to form a knob which he would round and smooth almost to perfection. The lad would then spend many hours each day throwing the rod until he could do it with lightning-like speed and almost perfect accuracy.

Philip Keller said,

> Some of my most vivid boyhood recollections are those of watching the African herdsmen shepherding their stock with only a long slender stick and a rough *knob-kerrie* [a short wooden club with a knob at one end used as a missile or in close attack especially by Zulus of southern Africa] in their hands. These are the common and universal equipment of the primitive sheepman. . . .
>
> I used to watch the native lads having competitions to see who could throw his rod with the greatest accuracy across the greatest distance. The effectiveness of these crude clubs in the hand of skilled shepherds was a thrill to watch. The rod was, in fact, an extension of the owner's

own right arm. It stood as a symbol of his strength, his power, his authority in any serious situation.[13]

Keller's statement, "the rod was . . . an extension of the owner's own right arm," strengthens the accounts of many other writers who state that a shepherd never went anywhere without his rod attached to his side.

The rod could be used in close-up encounters or thrown a short distance, but another instrument, though not mentioned in Psalm 23, which served better for accuracy at a longer distance was the sling.

We read in Judges 20:16 about 700 chosen men who could sling stones at an "hair breadth" and not miss. We also know that David carried a sling and had the courage and ability to use it when needed.

A shepherd always carried his rod, and having his sling close at hand would be the same principle practiced in the settling of the old West, when a cowboy wouldn't think of going outside, fully dressed, without his six-shooter strapped to his side. He would also have a rifle in the scabbard of his saddle, just in case he needed a weapon with more accuracy at a longer range.

A little reading between the lines in 1 Samuel 17 will show a strong probability that sometime earlier, David had used his rod to slay a lion and a bear. We know for sure he slew Goliath with his sling and a stone, but the close-up encounter with the lion and bear required a stronger weapon.

I can't imagine David holding the bear or lion with one hand while he beat them to death with the other, but we can imagine him

13. *The Shepherd Trilogy*, 82–83.

holding them with one hand while he beat the life out of them with his rod that was made for that very purpose. (See 1 Samuel 17:34–36.)

In addition to using the rod for protection, a sheepmaster could use it when purchasing new sheep to separate the wool and inspect the quality of the sheep's skin. It could also be used by the shepherd for taking inventory of his own sheep (see Leviticus 27:32), and when he saw something irregular in a sheep's appearance, he could use the rod to separate the wool searching for an injury or disease such as the common "scab," referred to earlier. The rod could also be dipped in a pot of dye and raked down the side of a sheep which was marked for the kill.

Did the shepherd break the lamb's leg?

Before moving away from our emphasis on the shepherd's rod, I will mention a frequently given report on the use of the rod that has made a lot of good preaching, but it is more than likely just grapevine news with no validity.

It has been said that a shepherd at times would break the leg of a consistently wandering lamb and then give that lamb special attention while the healing took place. By the time the leg had healed, the lamb would love the shepherd so strongly it would want to stay close to him for the rest of its life.

Since this report was so common in sermons on Psalm 23, I did extensive research but didn't find one documented case where a shepherd ever broke a lamb's leg with a rod, or any other instrument.

I did read a report in a book of sermons published in 1918 that referred to another book with the account of a shepherd breaking a lamb's leg. When I located that book I found these words—

> *I once heard* of a Scottish shepherd who was sorely tried by the frequent misadventures of one wild lamb. It gave more trouble than all the flock. It seemed incorrigible. One day the shepherd took that lamb and deliberately broke its leg.[14]

So, somebody said, that somebody else said, "I once heard of . . ." That doesn't go very far in trying to establish a fact. We can find no evidence that shepherds would break their sheep's legs to stop them from wandering, but we can find scriptural reasons why a lamb's leg should not be broken. According to Exodus 12:43–47 and Numbers 9:12, if a lamb had a broken bone it could not be a part of the Passover Feast. This would also eliminate it from being a type of our Passover lamb, the Lord Jesus Christ, for the Scriptures declare,

> Then came the soldiers, and brake the legs of the first, and of the other which was crucified with him. But when they came to Jesus, and saw that he was dead already, they brake not his legs: For these things were done, that the scripture should be fulfilled, A bone of him shall not be broken. (John 19:32–33, 36)

The staff

The shepherd's staff was much thinner, longer, and lighter than the rod, and like the rod served multiple purposes. Because of this

14. Freeman, *Life in the Uplands*, 73.

195

the staff was also very useful—sometimes as a walking stick to help the steps of the shepherd through rough or slippery terrain—sometimes to part the brush or briars when making a new path for the sheep—or sometimes to part the grass when searching for poisonous vipers. At other times, just a gentle tap of the staff on the side of a sheep looking the wrong direction would issue a warning to her not to go that way, and it would turn her back toward the flock.

When the staff became the shepherd's crook

Even though the term "shepherd's crook" or the word "crook" is not mentioned in the Bible, a study of the history of a shepherd's life in Israel will show that when the staff was bent on one end into a curve or had a curved piece of metal attached, it could be used to rescue a lamb or a sheep. (MacMillan, the Scottish shepherd, also claimed that sometimes a ram's horn was used to make the curve in the shepherd's crook.) The crook would be hooked around the leg or neck of a sheep which was caught in a thicket, had fallen into a ravine, or was in a similar situation, and then the animal could be pulled to safety. It could even be used for protection against vipers or less aggressive beasts.

Some claim the rod and the staff were only one instrument that was called a staff when the crook was at the end pointing toward the shepherd and was called a rod when pointing away from him.

The differences in the reports of the uses of the rod and the staff in shepherding usually come from different practices in different countries.

For example, here are the words of Douglas MacMillan, a very prominent Scottish preacher in his day, who "spent twelve years of his life as a shepherd on the Ardnamurchan peninsula in Argyll, the most westerly part of the Scottish mainland"[15]—

> Every commentator I have consulted has said that here is a shepherd going with a stick in one hand and a club in the other. . . . I never in my life saw a shepherd go to the hills with two crooks [sticks]; by the time they reached the stage when they needed two sticks, we used to say to them, "Just you stay at home!"[16]

MacMillan was very adamant (as are some writers from other countries) about the shepherds having only one instrument that served for both a rod and staff, but the Scriptures are very clear that the shepherds in ancient Israel had a rod *and* a staff.

Do the rod and staff bring comfort?

The rod and staff, without the skill, strength, and concern of the shepherd for the sheep, were of no value, but just one little word used in Psalm 23 two times made all the difference in the world—*thy* rod and *thy* staff. In fact, when danger was near, the sheep cast their eyes in the direction of the shepherd and didn't even take notice of the rod and the staff.

---

15. MacMillan, *The Lord Our Shepherd*, 8.
16. Ibid, 112.

The Lord Is My Shepherd, and That's Enough

I didn't notice.

History records that Cyrus, the founder of the Persian Empire, once had captured a prince and his family. When they came before him, the monarch asked the prisoner, "What will you give me if I release you?" "The half of my wealth," was his reply. "And if I release your children?" "Everything I possess." "And if I release your wife?" "Your Majesty, I will give myself."

Cyrus was so moved by his devotion that he freed them all. As they returned home, the prince said to his wife, "Wasn't Cyrus a handsome man!" With a look of deep love for her husband, she said to him, "I didn't notice. I could only keep my eyes on you—the one who was willing to give himself for me."[17]

As we make the application of this passage to New Testament truth, we will consider the shepherd's two items—the rod and the staff, which are types of the Word of God and the Holy Spirit, and we will see that both agents will point us to Christ, and thereby bring great comfort to the heart of the believer.

The Power of the Word of God

There is no way possible to know the Good Shepherd who gave His life for the sheep, which translates into "the gospel . . . by which ye are saved" (1 Corinthians 15:1–2), without the Scriptures.

Being born again, not of corruptible seed, but of incorruptible, by the word of God, which liveth and abideth

---

17. Jenkins, *The Kingdom Exposed*, 55.

for ever. For all flesh *is* as grass, and all the glory of man
as the flower of grass. The grass withereth, and the flower
thereof falleth away: But the word of the Lord endureth
for ever. And this is the word which by the gospel is
preached unto you. (1 Peter 1:23–25)

A New Testament passage that has been the text for thousands of
gospel sermons is Ephesians 2:8—"For by grace are ye saved through
faith," coupled with Romans 10:17—"So then faith *cometh* by hearing, and hearing by the word of God." Once we, as poor, undeserving
sinners, come to repentance toward God and faith in our Lord Jesus
Christ, we even find comfort in all the great Old Testament passages that point (through types and shadows) to Christ, our Good
Shepherd and the substance of our salvation.

> For whatsoever things were written aforetime were
> written for our learning, that we through patience and
> **comfort of the scriptures** might have hope. (Romans
> 15:4) (See also Colossians 2:16–17 and Hebrews 8:1–5;
> 10:1–7.)

There used to be an old song that we seldom hear sung anymore
entitled "Somewhere in the Shadows, You'll Find Jesus."

> Are your crosses too heavy to carry;
> And burdens too heavy to bear?
> Are there heartaches and tears and anguish;
> And there's no one who seems to care?
>
> Are there shadows of deep disappointment,
> And trusts that have proven untrue?

Has the darkness of night settled round you
Has your hope and your faith wavered too?

Has the storm overshadowed your sunshine,
And life lost attraction for you?
Have the dreams that you cherished been broken,
Is your soul filled with bitterness too?

Standing somewhere in the shadows you'll find Jesus,
He's the Friend who always cares and understands.
Standing somewhere in the shadows you will find Him
And you'll know Him by the nailprints in His hands.[18]

An actor converted

The following intriguing story that illustrates the power of the Word of God, comes from J. K. Johnston in his book, *Why Christians Sin*—

> Many years ago in a Moscow theater, matinee idol Alexander Rostovzev was converted while playing the role of Jesus in a sacrilegious play entitled *Christ in a Tuxedo*. He was supposed to read two verses from the Sermon on the Mount, remove his gown, and cry out, "Give me my tuxedo and top hat!" But as he read the words, "Blessed are the poor in spirit, for theirs is the kingdom of heaven. Blessed are they that mourn, for they shall be **comforted**," he began to tremble. Instead of following the script, he kept reading from Matthew 5, ignoring the coughs, calls,

18. E. J. Rollings

and foot-stamping of his fellow actors. Finally, recalling a verse he had learned in his childhood in a Russian Orthodox church, he cried, "Lord, remember me when Thou comest into Thy kingdom!" (Luke 23:42). Before the curtain could be lowered, Rostovzev had trusted Jesus Christ as his personal Saviour.[19]

The other agent is the Spirit of God—

"But the **Comforter,** *which is* the Holy Ghost, whom the Father will send in my name, he shall teach you all things, and bring all things to your remembrance, whatsoever I have said unto you." (John 14:26) (See also John 14:16; 15:26; and 16:7.)

One of the most amazing truths one will find in their study of the person and work of the Holy Spirit is how He always works in absolute union with the Scriptures. In fact, you will never find one word of discord between the two. For that reason we can confidently say, "the Word of God and the Spirit of God are working partners with the same purpose and goal," and when they work together the results will always be Christ-exalting and life-changing, but to try to use either and ignore the other is vain.

A ministerial student may study systematic theology through the lectures of a professor in a classroom and pass all the tests with remarkable grades, which can be a good thing. But, if the student, along with anyone else that carries the title "preacher," never learns and experiences the transforming power of the Holy Spirit and never allows Him to guide him into all truth, though he may spend many

19. 121.

years in the ministry and preach thousands of sermons, he will have a lack of faith in what he preaches. Even if he never reveals this in his preaching, it will be there.

Jesus told the disciples He was going away and that He would send the Holy Ghost, whom He called the Comforter, back to abide with them forever. In the first chapter of Acts, we read how Jesus defied the law of gravity and "went up" into Heaven.

The disciples may have lived for the next few days with perfect faith in the promise Jesus had made, but knowing human nature, some of them might have secretly questioned in their own hearts whether He made it back up to Heaven or not. But when the day of Pentecost was fully come, the Holy Spirit, whom Jesus said He would send, descended on them in Jerusalem and took up His abode in their hearts. From that moment on the disciples knew Jesus had made it all the way Home.

He is alive!

Gordon Brownville's book, *Symbols of the Holy Spirit,* tells about Roald Amundsen, the great Norwegian explorer, who discovered the magnetic meridian of the North Pole and discovered the South Pole. He took a homing pigeon with him on one of his trips, and released it when he had arrived at his destination. When his wife, back in Norway, looked up from the doorway of her home and saw the pigeon circling, she exclaimed, "He is alive!"

So, also, after Jesus had ascended, his disciples clung to his promise to send the Holy Spirit. They had great joy when the dove-like Holy Spirit descended at Pentecost. He was the continual reminder that Jesus was alive and victorious at the right hand of the Father. This continues to be the Spirit's message.[20]

The desire of every preacher should be to shun dead theology and preach a living Gospel, and this can only be done with both the Word of God and the Spirit of God. As Paul said in 1 Thessalonians 1:5, "For our gospel came not unto you in word only, but also in power, and in the Holy Ghost, and in much assurance."

As further proof that the *Word of God* and the *Spirit of God* work together in perfect harmony, notice the similarity between the following two passages of Scripture. One emphasizes the work of the Spirit of God, and the other emphasizes the work of the Word of God—

> And be not drunk with wine, wherein is excess; but be **filled with the Spirit**; Speaking to yourselves in psalms and hymns and spiritual songs, singing and making melody in your heart to the Lord; Giving thanks always for all things unto God and the Father in the name of our Lord Jesus Christ. (Ephesians 5:18–20)

and,

> **Let the word of Christ dwell in you richly** in all wisdom; teaching and admonishing one another in psalms and hymns and spiritual songs, singing with grace in your hearts to the Lord. And whatsoever ye do in word or deed, *do* all in the name of the Lord Jesus, giving thanks to God and the Father by him. (Colossians 3:16–17)

20. 25.

For me thy board is richly spread
In sight of all my foes,
Fresh oil of Thine embalms my head,
My cup of grace o'erflows.

Psalm 23:5

"Thou preparest a table before me in the presence of mine enemies: thou anointest my head with oil; my cup runneth over."

The way God treated David was the way David tried to treat the sheep. When we go back to Psalm 23:2 and read how David led the sheep into green pastures and beside the still waters, we understand he literally prepared a table for them; not only with an ample supply of food, but with enough left over for them to lie down in. Spurgeon wrote, "There is no fear of biting the bare ground where the grass is long enough for the flock to lie down in it."[1]

David now declares in verse five, "Thou [referring to 'The LORD [who] *is* my [his] shepherd' of verse 1] preparest a table before me in the presence of mine enemies."

We know David prepared the table for his sheep, and we know that "The LORD" (the Shepherd in Heaven) had prepared the table for David, but we are now on New Testament ground. Here the Shepherd in Heaven has come to earth in the person of our Good Shepherd, the Lord Jesus Christ, and while some are still speaking against God and asking, "Can God furnish a table in the wilderness?" (Psalm 78:19), we report with great joy that the table for us has already been prepared.

---

1. *The Treasury of David*, 354.

The Devil and His Henchmen

The preparation was made when Jesus invaded the devil's territory. After all, the devil is called the "god of this world" (2 Corinthians 4:4), and when Jesus was hanging in the atmosphere between Heaven and earth where the demonic powers reside, He overcame the prince of the powers of the air (Ephesians 2:2). The writer of Hebrews declares,

> Forasmuch then as the children are partakers of flesh and blood, he also himself likewise took part of the same; that through death he might destroy him that had the power of death, that is, the devil. (Hebrews 2:14)

This present evil world is a "wilderness," infested with the enemies of Christ and His sheep. Guy King described the devil and his cohorts with a few choice words—

> "That old serpent" (Revelation 12:9); "wolves" (Luke 10:3); "dogs" (Philippians 3:2); "a roaring lion" (1 Peter 5:8); and in John 10:1–13 we are warned against . . . the *open enemy*—the "wolf," . . . the *secret enemy*—the "thief," and . . . the *false friend*—the "hireling."[2]

To take the time to try and locate, identify, and describe all of the enemies would be a waste of time and space because it doesn't make any difference who they are, where they are, or how many there are—their leader has already been defeated, and in my imagination I can see "the devil, as a roaring lion, [walking] about, **seeking whom he may devour**." (1 Peter 5:8), but each and every one of Christ's sheep has already been sealed and marked for safe delivery.

---

2. *All Through the Day*, 70.

Romans 8:32 declares, "He that spared not his own Son, but delivered him up for us all, how shall he not with him also freely give us all things?" The words "all things" surely include a table in the wilderness.

The King's Table

A good illustration of one being brought to the shepherd/king's table and being given a total supply for all of his needs is in the intriguing story of David bringing Mephibosheth from the land of Lodebar (which means "no pastures") to his palace. If there are no pastures, there will be no sheep or shepherds.

We read in 2 Samuel 4:4,

> And Jonathan, Saul's son, had a son *that was* lame of *his* feet. He was five years old . . . and his nurse took him up, and fled: and it came to pass, as she made haste to flee, that he fell, and became lame. And his name *was* Mephibosheth.

King David had compassion on this one who was lame through the fall of another and was living in a land of no bread, or as some would say, "a land of forgotten people." He sent a servant to fetch him, and when Mephibosheth came before King David,

> he fell on his face, and did reverence. And David said, Mephibosheth. And he answered, Behold thy servant! And David said unto him, **Fear not**: for I will surely shew thee kindness for Jonathan thy father's sake, and will **restore** thee all the land of Saul thy father; and **thou shalt eat bread at my table continually**. . . . Then the king

called to Ziba, . . . and said unto him, . . . thy sons, and thy servants, shall till the land for him, and thou shalt bring *in the fruits*, that [he] may have food to eat: but **Mephibosheth thy master's son shall eat bread alway at my table.** . . . As for Mephibosheth, *said the king,* **he shall eat at my table**, as one of the king's sons. . . . And all that dwelt in the house of Ziba *were* servants unto Mephibosheth. So Mephibosheth dwelt in Jerusalem: for **he did eat continually at the king's table**; and was lame on both his feet. (2 Samuel 9:6–13)

Four times in this chapter we are told that Mephibosheth did *eat bread at the king's table* (See verses 7, 10–11, and 13). It is also recorded that he became a big landowner with thirty-six servants (See verses 7 and 10).

If all that was included in the privilege of sitting at the king's table was three square meals each day, there would have been no need for Mephibosheth to become a landowner with all of those servants. It's very clear that David, the shepherd/king, made sure that not only was there physical food for him in abundance, but that every other need that he had was taken care of.

Now, we Christians can rejoice, not just in the beautiful, poetical terms of Psalm 23 or just in the many dramatic illustrations or just in the songs that have been composed, but in the reality that the table these things point to, has been spread for us.

The hymn writer C. B. Widmeyer was right, when back in 1907, he wrote,

Jesus has a table spread
Where the saints of God are fed,
He invites His chosen people, "Come and dine";
With His manna He doth feed
And supplies our every need:
Oh, 'tis sweet to sup with Jesus all the time![3]

Thou anointest my head with oil

Sheep diseases and treatments

There are many diseases that sheep get easily, but two very common ones are "scab," and fly infestations from "fly strikes."

Scab

Sheep scab, or *psoroptic mange,* also called "wet mange," is a very contagious disease caused by mites feeding on the surface layers of the skin. A sheep with scab will experience severe itching, their wool or hair will fall out in patches, and the skin will be reddened and encrusted with scabs.

Flies

Blowflies strike the flesh of living sheep by laying eggs on them. The larvae (also called wool maggots or fleece worms) then hatch and bury themselves below the wool, then below the skin, feeding off their flesh. Sheep are usually affected easier than other animals because of their wool. Dirty wool especially attracts blowflies.

3. "Come and Dine," stanza 1.

For the treatment of these maggots, most shepherd writers tell us of large vats filled with water which has been treated with an efficient amount of a concentrated chemical solution they use to dip the sheep. It is very effective in curing the diseases and insects in the wool or on the skin of the sheep, but they need a different remedy for the flies around the sheep's head.

Nose flies

Nasal bots, bot flies, or head bots are most commonly called "nose flies." They deposit living larvae (maggots) on the mucus membranes of the sheep's nose. These eggs hatch in a few days and form a small, slender, worm-like larvae. These larvae then work their way up the nasal passage into the sheep's head and burrow into the flesh, causing an intense irritation accompanied by severe inflammation and in some cases even blindness.

Many times when a fly strike first occurs, the sheep stand with their heads to the ground trying to avoid the attack of the flies, but once the infestation takes place, the sheep may beat their heads against trees, rocks, or brush for relief from their agony. In extreme cases they have been known to kill themselves in order to get relief.

Failing methods of fly control

One method of trying to control "nose flies" that was used by some sheep ranchers in early America was to split a log so the top half would be flat. They then drilled several holes into the log deep enough to hold a good supply of salt and big enough for the sheep to eat the salt out of the hole. The outer rim of the hole was then coated with a coal tar-like substance so that the sheep would get its nose treated with the "fly repellent" every time it ate the salt.

The tar around the sheep's nose would provide a partial repellent for the "nose flies," but it would never be a complete fix because there would always be sheep that never ate the salt. Also, there were many other insects such as gnats, ticks, mosquitoes, and a large variety of other flies that would still agitate the sheep.

Another method of fly control was to hang a curtain of burlap or similar heavy material soaked with an oily repellent at a point in the path of the sheep so there was only a narrow passage for them to go through. As the sheep passed through that narrow opening, the curtain would drag across the sheep's back so a few flies and other insects would be eliminated.

In more modern times some shepherds would hang "fly strips" (long, narrow strips of paper or plastic coated with a sticky substance) that would trap the flies legs when they landed on them, thus eliminating many flies. But regardless of how many different man-made remedies or brands of repellents have flooded the "farmer's market," nothing can improve on the way David did it.

Oil for the ram's head

Before we pursue the subject of fly control further, another use for the oil was to pour it over the ram's head. Rams would fight for the top position among the ewes, and when they ran and hit their heads together, their horns might be broken or their heads split open. Sometimes a ram would even be killed. To remedy the problem the shepherd would pour oil over their heads, and when they hit each other, they would slide off with very little harm done.

He touched me!

Sheep, being very affectionate animals, loved to feel the touch of their master's hand as he lovingly and tenderly rubbed their head and talked to them. Shepherds with flocks small enough, such as David's obviously was (see 1 Samuel 17:28), would give personal and special attention to each and every one. In my meditation on this scene, I can now see the shepherd pouring the oil over the top of the sheep's head. With his hands he gently rubbed it into every fold of the skin, around the ears and eyes, and under the neck, making sure he had completely covered every spot on its head.

When the sheep's head had been totally *saturated* with the oil, some would begin to drip from the bottom of its chin. One writer says that in some cases a catch-pan would be placed under the sheep's head to catch the excess oil as it dripped from its chin. When an observer would see the excess oil in the catch-pan, he would know the shepherd had done "exceeding abundantly above" all that was needed to protect the sheep's head from the attack of the flies.

If sheep could sing, we might have heard them after they had felt the touch of the shepherd's hand and been anointed with oil, joyfully singing the chorus of that old American children's song as they went running back into the flock—

Shoo fly, don't bother me
Shoo fly, don't bother me

Shoo fly, don't bother me
I belong to somebody

The flies that attack the head of the sheep are a type of evil, demonic spirits that try to get into the mind of every person. If they succeed they will bring untold suffering, and like some sheep being tormented to the point of killing themselves, some people even become suicidal.

When Jesus cast a devil out of a man that was dumb, His critics said, "He casteth out devils through **Beelzebub** the chief of the devils" (Luke 11:15).

> The name "Beelzebub," written also "Beelzebul," which occurs nowhere else in Jewish literature, is a variant form of "Baal Zebub," the god of Ekron, whose oracle King Ahaziah consulted during his illness, provoking thereby the wrath of God (2 Kings 1:2–16); . . . the name is commonly explained . . . as the "*Lord of Flies*" (see Baal-zebub). . . . The fly was regarded by the Jews in particular as more or less impure and demonic.[4]

No truly, born-again Christian will ever be destroyed by demon possession, but as noted in an earlier chapter, one may recognize the Saviour of Psalm 22 and become a saved, blood-bought child of God, but fail to see himself as a helpless sheep in Psalm 23, totally dependent on the Good Shepherd for His care and protection. If that happens to be your condition, the devil knows that he will never drag your soul into hell. He knows that you have eternal life, and he can't do anything about it, but he will look for every opportunity to

---

4. Kohler, "BEELZEBUB or BEELZEBUL," *The Jewish Encyclopedia*, 629–30.

keep you from living the "abundant life"—a life filled with peace and contentment illustrated in this Twenty-third Psalm.

When the devil sets out to deceive and defeat you as a Christian, he will always send one or more of his evil spirits to attack your mind through outward influences. It will usually be through what you see or hear, and he will tempt you to walk after the old, Adamic nature—a fruitless, miserable life of carnality and selfishness.

Also, keep in mind that one day you will come face to face with the One who loved you and gave Himself for you. When you see Him, how ashamed you will be for living such a self-centered life, especially when the abundant life was available.

How can I have this abundant life of peace and contentment?

Just like there are no man-made methods of total fly control with sheep, there are no programs, methods, or works of the flesh you can perform to assure you of a victorious, Christian life. You cannot defeat your adversary, the devil, on your own—you cannot manufacture the Holy Spirit—you cannot fill yourself. However, you have been given the option of living a self-centered life filled with greed, heartache, and defeat, or living a peaceful, contented, righteous, and productive life "for his name's sake."

The hymn writer, Frances Havergal, surely knew something of a life lived *for His name sake* when she wrote,

> Take my life and let it be
> Consecrated, Lord, to Thee.

Take my moments and my days,
Let them flow in endless praise.

Take my hands and let them move
At the impulse of Thy love.
Take my feet and let them be
Swift and beautiful for Thee.

Take my voice and let me sing,
Always, only for my King.
Take my lips and let them be
Filled with messages from Thee.

Take my silver and my gold,
Not a mite would I withhold.
Take my intellect and use
Every pow'r as Thou shalt choose.

Take my will and make it Thine,
It shall be no longer mine.
Take my heart, it is Thine own,
It shall be Thy royal throne.

Take my love, my Lord, I pour
At Thy feet its treasure store.
Take myself and I will be
Ever, only, all for Thee.[5]

In our weakness, none of us have the ability within ourselves to live day by day, moment by moment for Christ and Him alone; we

5. Frances Havergal, "Take My Life and Let It Be."

must be anointed, saturated, filled, led, controlled, and empowered for service by the Holy Ghost. But how can it be?

When a person makes their personal consecration to the Good Shepherd, as David did when he said, "The LORD *is* my shepherd," all of the blessings in the last five verses become theirs—including being anointed with oil.

It's so simple!

When you simply recognize your human weakness and acknowledge Christ as your Good Shepherd, you will have no need to concern yourself about how to be anointed with the Holy Ghost. The Shepherd will take care of that for you.

My cup runneth over

Much speculation has been offered about what the cup could represent. Some writers suggest the shepherd allowed the sheep to drink from his own cup or from a large stone pot. Then when the sheep would plunge its nose into the water, some of it would overflow, and from that David saw an analogy of the blessings of God on his life. This illustration, at best is very weak because David said "my cup" runneth over, not the shepherd's cup, and in the verse we are dealing with oil rather than water.

Another, very popular view is that "my cup runneth over" refers to the hospitality of an oriental host.

The following experience of Captain James Wilson, is found in his *Memoirs*, published in the early 1800s—

I once had this ceremony performed to me. . . . The gentleman of the house poured upon my hands and arms a delightful odoriferous perfume, put a golden cup into my hand, and poured wine into it, till it ran over, assuring me at the same time that it was a great pleasure to him to receive me, and that I should find a rich supply [of my needs] in his house.[6]

This illustration of the hospitality of an oriental host certainly does find its type in the overflowing cup, but was that what David was referring to? I think not!

In these words David was giving a summary of all the blessings from the Shepherd mentioned in the previous verses, and being overwhelmed with the Shepherd and His supply. To paraphrase David's statement, he was saying, "I have received so many benefits that I cannot contain them all"; "My cup runneth over"; and now that David's Shepherd has become our Shepherd, He continually proves Himself to be more than enough, day after day, by filling our cup with so many blessings that our cup "runneth over."

With Him the calf is always the fatted calf; the robe is always the best robe; the joy is unspeakable; the peace passeth understanding; the grace is so abundant that the recipient has all-sufficiency for all things, and abounds in every good work. There is no grudging in God's benevolence. He does not measure out His goodness as the apothecary counts his drops and measures his drams, slowly and exactly, drop by drop.

6. Griffin, *Memoirs of Captain James Wilson*, 66.

God's way is always characterized by . . . overflowing bounty, like that in nature, which is so profuse with beauty and life that every drop of the ocean, and every square inch of the forest glade, and every molecule of matter teems with marvels, and defies the research and investigation of man. . . .

But it is especially in connection with spiritual blessing that the cup most often seems to overflow. This has been the experience of many eminent saints. In one of his seasons of rapt communion, John Welch, of Scotland, cried, "O Lord, Hold thy hand; it is enough. Thy servant is a clay vessel, and can contain no more!" . . .

Certain it is that our Lord Jesus meant for us to have a more abiding experience of such joys. He not only came to give us life, but life more abundantly. He spake unto us His inimitable [matchless] words, that our joy might be full. He meant our hearts to delight themselves with fatness, and to be satisfied with the favor of the Lord.[7]

---

7. Meyer, *The Shepherd Psalm*, 63–64.

O nought but love and mercy wait
Through all my life on me,
And I within my Father's gate
For long bright years shall be.

Psalm 23:6

"Surely goodness and mercy shall follow me all the days of my life: and I will dwell in the house of the LORD for ever."

What about Sheep Dogs?

As time went on many changes were made in the way shepherds prepared for the needs of their sheep. Many were grazed on privately owned, fenced property and sheep dogs replaced the sling, the rod, and the staff. Keller said, "One good sheep dog and myself could accomplish as much as five men."[1]

Different shepherds may prefer one breed over another, but those familiar with the border collie tell us they have the nature for keeping sheep bunched together that only God could give them. This "herding" instinct has even been shown by the true account of a border collie kept inside as a family pet who tried to push all the furniture together into the middle of a room.

The following words also shed light on how useful the sheep dog can be—

> Dogs aid the shepherd in caring for the sheep. Dogs love the sheep, but hate the sheep's enemies. Dogs carefully guard against danger. If a sheep lags behind the flock, the dog brings it up near the shepherd. If a sheep runs

1. Keller, *Lessons from a Sheep Dog*, 1.

ahead it is brought back to where the shepherd desires that the sheep feed. If it wanders to the right or to the left of the chosen path, the dogs will see that it returns to the place of following the shepherd. Toward any foe of the sheep, these dogs have a fierce attitude. Toward the sheep and the shepherd, they have an attitude of love and faithfulness.[2]

I readily admit that much more could be learned through a study of the nature and intelligence of the sheep dog, and for those interested in more insight into the ability of these amazing creatures, I recommend you begin your research by reading two fabulous books—*Do Border Collies Dream of Sheep?* by Carol Lea Benjamin and C. Denise Wall and *Lessons From a Sheep Dog, A True Story of Transforming Love,* by Phillip Keller. However, even though many modern-day shepherds declare that a well-trained dog from the right breed is the best friend a sheep can have, I have overcome my temptation to include a chapter in this book entitled, *Do Border Collies Laugh At People?* and leave the study of canines to those writers who view goodness and mercy as "two hounds from Heaven" or "two heavenly sheep dogs sent to follow the flock."

Goodness and Mercy

When the psalmist said, "Surely goodness and mercy shall follow me all the days of my life," he was expressing two very important truths that all of us would do well to embrace.

---

2. Gaddis, *The Shepherd Psalm,* 41–42.

First, David never expected to reach a state of sinless perfection in his lifetime. There are those who teach a "second work of grace" and hold a heretical view of the "baptism of the Holy Ghost" in which the old Adamic nature is supposedly eradicated and that they never sin again. If that doctrine were true, there would be no need for mercy beyond the point of that make-believe experience.

Second, David intended on keeping short accounts with God, because the only way one can be assured of mercy is by confessing and forsaking sin and by shewing mercy to others—"He that covereth his sins shall not prosper: but whoso confesseth and forsaketh *them* shall have mercy" (Proverbs 28:13), and James 2:13 declares that "he shall have judgment without mercy, that hath shewed no mercy; and mercy rejoiceth against judgment."

When David penned Psalm 23, he had good intentions, but in later years that old Adamic nature got the best of him, and David's actions toward another man's wife are described by the words of the Apostle Paul, "For the good that I would I do not: but the evil which I would not, that I do" (Romans 7:19). As a young shepherd boy, David had no idea he would be the one to commit the sin that would be recorded in the Bible and used as a text for thousands of sermons warning against what many have called the "scarlet sin of adultery."

When we read, "Because David did *that which was* right in the eyes of the LORD, and turned not aside from any *thing* that he commanded him all the days of his life, save only in the matter of Uriah the Hittite" (1 Kings 15:5), one might have a tendency to downplay the severity of David's sin of adultery. But when we take a look at the actual account as recorded in 2 Samuel 11, and the results that followed in the next three chapters, we are once more reminded that God is no respecter of persons—even the king will be judged for his sins.

If the reader doubts the severity of God toward sin, read these somber words—

And Nathan said to David,…Thus saith the LORD God of Israel, I anointed thee king over Israel, and I delivered thee out of the hand of Saul; And I gave thee thy master's house, and thy master's wives into thy bosom, and gave thee the house of Israel and of Judah; and if *that had been* too little, I would moreover have given unto thee such and such things. Wherefore hast thou despised the commandment of the LORD, to do evil in his sight? thou hast killed Uriah the Hittite with the sword, and hast taken his wife *to be* thy wife, and hast slain him with the sword of the children of Ammon. Now therefore the sword shall never depart from thine house; because thou hast despised me, and hast taken the wife of Uriah the Hittite to be thy wife. Thus saith the LORD, Behold, I will raise up evil against thee out of thine own house, and I will take thy wives before thine eyes, and give *them* unto thy neighbour, and he shall lie with thy wives in the sight of this sun. For thou didst *it* secretly: but I will do this thing before all Israel, and before the sun. And David said unto Nathan, I have sinned against the LORD. And Nathan said unto David, The LORD also hath put away thy sin; thou shalt not die. Howbeit, because by this deed thou hast given great occasion to the enemies of the LORD to blaspheme, the child also *that is* born unto thee shall surely die. (2 Samuel 12:7–14)

In the following chapters we read about the death of David's baby (12:18), his daughter Tamar being raped by her own brother (13:1–14), the murder of one son by another son (13:28–29), and the plot of Absalom to dethrone his own father (15:1–6).

Some commentators also believe when David said,

There is no soundness in my flesh because of thine anger; neither *is there any* rest in my bones because of my sin. . . . My wounds stink *and* are corrupt because of my foolishness. . . . For my loins are filled with a loathsome *disease*: and *there is* no soundness in my flesh. . . . My lovers and my friends stand aloof from my sore; and my kinsmen stand afar off. (Psalm 38:3, 5, 7, 11)

that he was describing a venereal disease that he carried for the rest of his life as part of God's judgment on his sin.

To say the least, David suffered drastically because of his folly, but let's now take another view of the situation—

And the LORD sent Nathan unto David. And he came unto him, and said unto him, There were two men in one city; the one rich, and the other poor. The rich *man* had exceeding many flocks and herds: But the poor *man* had nothing, save one little ewe lamb, which he had bought and nourished up: and it grew up together with him, and with his children; it did eat of his own meat, and drank of his own cup, and lay in his bosom, and was unto him as a daughter. And there came a traveller unto the rich man, and he spared to take of his own flock and of his own herd, to dress for the wayfaring man that was come unto him; but took the poor man's lamb, and dressed it for the man that was come to him. And David's anger was greatly kindled against the man; and he said to Nathan, *As* the LORD liveth, the man that hath done this *thing* shall surely die: And he shall restore the lamb fourfold, because he did this thing, and because **he had no pity.** And Nathan said to David, **Thou *art* the man.** (2 Samuel 12:1–7)

Nathan gave the parable to reveal the condition of David's heart, and when David said, "He shall restore the lamb fourfold," he was showing that if the parable had been a real life situation, he would have made no effort to restore the one who had been overtaken in the fault—David showed no pity, compassion, or mercy while trying to keep his own sin covered (like plucking the mote out of your brother's eye when there is a beam in your own), but thankfully, in later years, he came clean with God and said, "For I *am* ready to halt, and my sorrow *is* continually before me. For I will declare mine iniquity; I will be sorry for my sin" (Psalm 38:17–18).

Then, in what is referred to by many as a penitential psalm, David said,

Have mercy upon me, O God, according to thy loving-kindness: according unto the multitude of thy tender mercies blot out my transgressions. Wash me throughly from mine iniquity, and cleanse me from my sin. For

I acknowledge my transgressions: and my sin *is* ever before me. Against thee, thee only, have I sinned, and done *this* evil in thy sight: that thou mightest be justified when thou speakest, *and* be clear when thou judgest. Behold, I was shapen in iniquity; and in sin did my mother conceive me. Behold, thou desirest truth in the inward parts: and in the *hidden* part thou shalt make me to know wisdom. Purge me with hyssop, and I shall be clean: wash me, and I shall be whiter than snow. Make me to hear joy and gladness; *that* the bones *which* thou hast broken may rejoice. Hide thy face from my sins, and blot out all mine iniquities. Create in me a clean heart, O God; and renew a right spirit within me. Cast me not away from thy presence; and take not thy holy spirit from me. Restore unto me the joy of thy salvation; and uphold me *with thy* free spirit. *Then* will I teach transgressors thy ways; and sinners shall be converted unto thee. Deliver me from bloodguiltiness, O God, thou God of my salvation: *and* my tongue shall sing aloud of thy righteousness. O Lord, open thou my lips; and my mouth shall shew forth thy praise. For thou desirest not sacrifice; else would I give *it*: thou delightest not in burnt offering. The sacrifices of God *are* a broken spirit: a broken and a contrite heart, O God, thou wilt not despise. (Psalm 51:1–17)

Once David had confessed his sin with a repentant heart and cried out for mercy, his sins were forgiven and his fellowship restored. Even his son Solomon testified of the mercy shown when he said unto God, "Thou hast shewed great mercy unto David my father, and hast made me to reign in his stead" (2 Chronicles 1:8).

Here is something better than angel help: the personified attributes of God, His goodness, His mercy; that is, Himself, in all the tenderest manifestations of His love and pity towards men.

Goodness AND Mercy. Not goodness alone, for we are sinners needing forgiveness. Not mercy alone, for we need many things besides forgiveness. . . .

Goodness to supply every want, mercy to forgive every sin; goodness to provide, mercy to pardon. David often links these two together, as when he says, "The LORD *is* good; His mercy *is* everlasting" [Psalm 100:5]. What shall we say of these blessed attributes? Take Goodness. It is laid up in vast reservoirs in the nature of God. . . .

Take Mercy. She is the daughter of God: His delight, "He delighteth *in* mercy" [Micah 7:18]; His wealth, ". . . rich in mercy" [Ephesians 2:4]; His throne, "I will commune with thee from above [off] the mercy seat" [Exodus 25:22].[3]

"All the days of my life" is a simple description of "the valley of the shadow of death." We are all traveling on the road of life, and Dr. John Phillips offered these encouraging and enlightening words—

We are given two glimpses . . . of *the King's highway.* We are on a journey. Hard on the heels come God's two

---

3. Meyer, *The Shepherd Psalm*, 67–68.

great ambassadors—goodness and mercy. Goodness takes care *my steps;* mercy takes care of *my stumbles.*[4]

I will dwell in the house of the LORD for ever

We now approach the closing statement of this psalm with a sense of inability to do it justice with our feeble comments, so we once again resort to the words of Dr. Meyer.

> The passing of the years awakens in our hearts the cry for permanence. . . . There arises up within us a passionate desire for a home which death cannot invade. . . .
>
> This permanence for which we wait seems promised in the words with which the shepherd minstrel closes the psalm, which are simple as the words "home" and "mother," and quite as full of meaning. . . .
>
> No doubt the changes of our mortal life are all needed to fit us for the changeless. Time is the necessary vestibule or robing-room for eternity. Earth is the training-house for the real life which awaits us when the last lesson is learned and the school-bell rings. . . .
>
> But better than the thought of permanence is the thought that heaven is a HOME; it is "the house of the Lord," which is the nearest approach possible in the Old Testament to the words of Jesus: "In my Father's house are many mansions."[5]

---

4. *Exploring Psalms,* 179.
5. *Shepherd Psalm,* 71–72.

There is great certainty in these words. The psalmist has no doubt that he will be there. Yet he had been
a wandering sheep; his record by no means stainless;
his temper rather that of a man of war and blood than
that of peace and gentleness and love, which would befit
the meek denizen [resident] of heaven. How should he
come there? And what made him so sure? He doubtless
felt that the Good Shepherd could not be there while the
sheep was bleating piteously without. "Where I am, there
ye shall be also." And we have a yet more sure word of
promise, to which we may joyfully take heed as to a light
which shines in a dark place.

Because we have trusted Christ and are one with
Him; because we have received into our hearts the germ
of eternal life, which carries with it heaven in embryo;
because we have the earnest of our inheritance already
in the presence and witness of the Holy Ghost; because
God's promise and oath assure us of our eternal bless-
edness, two things which make disappointment impos-
sible, for all these reasons and others, the humblest, most
timid, and weakest believer that reads these lines may
dare affirm, "I will dwell in the house of the Lord forever."[6]

How long is forever?

I once heard that great old preacher, Dr. Ralph Sexton, Sr., give
his view of forever in words like this—When time runs out, and the

6. Ibid., 74.

ages begin, God will be there to start them; and when the ages run into the ages of ages, God will be there to start them; and when the ages of ages run into the eons, God will be there to start the eons; and when the eons run into the eons of eons God will be there to start the eons of eons; and when they stagger home, tired and exhausted from their never ending task of everlastingness, God will be there to greet them and start them on another cycle of everlastingness.

Conclusion

If the reader can truly say "the LORD *is* my shepherd," and through the pages of this book has found another reason for loving Him more, then to God be all the glory. Our mission has been accomplished.

It's now time to end our study on this, in my opinion, greatest six verse section of Scripture in all of the Bible—not because there is no more information that could be included—but simply because the impression of my heart is "It's time to stop."

THE END

BIBLIOGRAPHY

Alcorn, Randy. "Shepherd Status." In *Come Thou Long Expected Jesus*, edited by Nancy Guthrie. Wheaton, IL: Crossway Books, 2008.

Barnes, Albert. *Barnes' New Testament Notes—Enhanced Version*. 1st ed. Christian Classics Ethereal Library, 2010. Kindle edition.

Beecher, Henry Ward. *Life Thoughts*. Complete First and Second Series. London: James Blackwood and Co.

Brownville, C. Gordon. *Symbols of the Holy Spirit*. Wheaton, IL: Tyndale House Publishers, 1978.

Chapman, J. Wilbur, D.D. *The Secret of a Happy Day*. Boston and Chicago: United Society of Christian Endeavor, 1899.

Clarke, Adam. *Clarke on the Whole Bible: Adam Clarke's Bible Commentary*. Kindle edition.

Dale, Thomas, M.A. *The Good Shepherd and the Chosen Flock: Shewing the Progress of the Sheep of Christ through the Wilderness of This World to the Pastures of the Heavenly Zion, An Exposition of the Twenty-third Psalm*. London: Bowdery and Kerby, 1845.

Emery, Allan C. *A Turtle on a Fencepost: Little Lessons of Great Importance*. Waco, TX: Word Books, 1979.

Evans, William. *The Shepherd Psalm: A Meditation*. Chicago, IL: The Bible Institute Colportage Association, 1921. Kindle.

Freeman, J. D. *Life on the Uplands: An Interpretation of the Twenty-third Psalm*. New York, NY: A. C. Armstrong & Son, 1907.

Gaddis, Tilden H. *The Shepherd Psalm*. Kansas City, MO: Nazarene Publishing House, 1936.

Griffin, John. *Memoirs of Captain James Wilson, Containing an Account of His Enterprises and Sufferings in India, His Conversion* to Christianity, His Missionary Voyage to the South Seas, and His Peaceful and Triumphant Death. 1st American ed. Boston: Samuel T. Armstrong, and Crocker & Brewster, 1822.

Jamieson, Robert, D.D. Eastern Manners Illustrative of the New Testament History. 3rd ed. Edinburgh: William Oliphant and Sons, 1852.

Jenkins, George. The Kingdom Exposed. Bloomington, IN: West Bow Press, 2012.

Johnston, J. K. Why Christians Sin. Discovery House, 1992.

Kanoy, J. William. Psalm 23. Louisville, KY: Colonial Baptist Press, 1988.

Keller, W. Phillip. A Shepherd Looks at the Good Shepherd and His Sheep. Grand Rapids, MI: Zondervan Publishing House, 1978.

Keller, W. Phillip. The Shepherd Trilogy. Grand Rapids, MI: Zondervan, 1996.

Keller, W. Phillip. Lessons from a Sheep Dog. Nashville, TN: Thomas Nelson, 2002.

Kennedy, Benjamin Hall, D.D. The Psalter or Psalms of David in English Verse. Cambridge: Deighton, Bell and Co., 1876.

Ker, John. Psalms in History and Biography. Classic Reprint. London, England: Forgotten Books, 2015.

Ketcham, Robert T. I Shall Not Want: An Exposition of Psalm Twenty-three. Chicago, IL: Moody Press, 1953.

King, Guy Hope. All through the Day: Meditations from the Twenty-third Psalm. Grand Rapids, MI: Zondervan Publishing House, 1980.

Knight, William Allen. *The Song of Our Syrian Guest*. 1904. http://www.gutenberg.org/cache/epub/12615/pg12615.html.

Kohler, Kaufmann. "BEELZEBUB or BEELZEBUL." *The Jewish Encyclopedia*. 1st ed. Vol. 2. New York & London: Funk and Wagnalls Company, 1906.

Lockaby, George W. *Salvation's Psalm 23*. 1975.

Lockyer, Herbert, Sr. *Psalms: A Devotional Commentary*. Grand Rapids, MI: Kregel, 1993.

Lucado, Max. *Safe in the Shepherd's Arms: Hope & Encouragement from Psalm 23*. Thomas Nelson, 2009.

Lyle, Denis. *From Earth to Glory: Comforting Thoughts from Psalm 23*. Christian Year Publications, 2017.

MacMillan, J. Douglas. *The Lord Our Shepherd*. Bridgend, Wales: Bryntirion Press, 2003.

McDonald, William, ed. *The Socialite Who Killed a Nazi with Her Bare Hands: And 143 Other Fascinating People Who Died This Past Year*. New York, NY: Workman Publishing Company, 2013.

McElwee, Bobby. *Psalm Twenty-Three: The "Pearl" of Psalms*. Danville, VA: Riverview Baptist Church, 1978.

Meikle, James. *Solitude Sweetened; or Miscellaneous Meditations on Various Religious Subjects, Written in Distant Parts of the World*. Milton, FL: Victory Baptist Press, 2010.

Meyer, F. B. *Shepherd Psalm*. Memphis, TN: Bottom of the Hill Publishing, 2011.

Morgan, Charles Herbert. *The Psalms as Daily Companions*. Chicago, IL: The Epworth League of the Methodist Episcopal Church, 1919.

Morgan, Jill. *A Man of the Word: Life of G. Campbell Morgan*. Eugine, OR: Wipf & Stock Publishers, 1951.

Nichols, Thomas McBride. *Preaching: A Series of Brief Chapters*. Milton, FL, Victory Baptist Press, 2017.

Phillips, John. *Exploring Psalms: An Expository Commentary*. Vol. 1. Grand Rapids, MI: Kregel Publications, 2002.

Prothero, Rowland E. *The Psalms in Human Life*. Vestavia Hills, AL: Solid Ground Christian Books, 1903.

Rogers, William Avery. *The Shepherd and His Sheep: An Exposition of Psalm 23*. Asheville, NC: Revival Literature, 1983.

Ruckman, Peter. *Psalms Commentary*. Vol. 1. The Bible Believer's Commentary Series. BB Bookstore, 2011.

Sankey, Ira D. *My Life Story and the Story of Gospel Hymns, Sacred Songs and Solos*. Milton, FL: Victory Baptist Press, 2012.

Shapiro, Rami M. *Rabbi Rami Guide to Psalm 23 & Jesus' Two Great Commandments: Roadside Assistance for the Spiritual Traveler*. Traverse City, MI: Spirituality & Health Publisher, 2011.

Simpson, John, and Edmund Weiner, eds. *The Oxford English Dictionary*. 2nd ed. Oxford, England: Clarendon Press, 1989.

Slemming, C. W. *He Leadeth Me: Shepherd Life in Palestine Psalm 23*. Fort Washington, PA: Christian Literature Crusade, 1973.

Spurgeon, Charles H. *The Treasury of David: Containing an Original Exposition of the Book of Psalms; a Collection of Illustrative Extracts from the Whole Range of Literature; a Series of Homiletical Hints upon Almost Every Verse; and Lists of Writers upon Each Psalm*. Vol. I. LVII vols. Peabody, MA: Hendrickson Publishers.

Stevenson, John. *The Lord Our Shepherd: An Exposition of the Twenty-third Psalm.* 1845.

Wentworth, Edward Norris. *America's Sheep Trails, History & Personalities.* Ames, IA: Iowa State College Press, 1948.